The Daily 5

FOSTERING LITERACY INDEPENDENCE IN THE ELEMENTARY GRADES

Second Edition

Stenhouse Publishers
Portland, Maine

Pembroke Publishers
Markham, Ontario

GAIL BOUSHEY & JOAN MOSER *"The 2 Sisters"*

Stenhouse Publishers
www.stenhouse.com

Pembroke Publishers
www.pembrokepublishers.com

Library of Congress Cataloging-in-Publication Data
Boushey, Gail, 1956–
    The daily 5 : fostering literacy independence in the elementary grades /
Gail Boushey and Joan Moser, "the 2 Sisters".—Second edition.
        pages cm
    Includes bibliographical references.
        ISBN 978-1-57110-974-3 (pbk. : alk. paper)—ISBN 978-1-62531-002-6
(ebook) 1. Language arts (Elementary) 2. Individualized instruction—Case
studies. I. Moser, Joan, 1962– II. Title.
        LB1576.B535 2014
        372.6—dc23
                                                                    2013031855

Cover design, interior design, and typesetting by Martha Drury
Front cover photograph and chapter opener photographs by Gelfand-Piper
Photography
Back cover photograph courtesy of Janel Gion Photography and Design
Manufactured in the United States of America

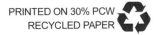
PRINTED ON 30% PCW
RECYCLED PAPER

20 19 18 17 16 15 14   9 8 7 6 5 4 3

**For our parents,
our first and forever teachers**

# Contents

Acknowledgments

Our development of the Daily 5 began over fifteen years ago. Between those first years and the writing of this second edition, many circles of support have surrounded us.

We are appreciative of all the professional conversations as well as the opportunities to capture student learning on film in the schools where we have taught: Crestline, Russell Academy, Meridian, Walt Disney, Green Gables, and Woodridge. Thank you for opening your classrooms and continuing to stretch our thinking.

Our work developing the Daily 5 expanded beyond the walls of our classrooms and schools to include teachers from all over the world who have read our books, attended our conferences and workshops, and subscribed to our website. We thank you. You make our teaching and our writing so much richer.

We are grateful to Margaret Mooney, who was the first person to challenge us to find a different way to create engaged and independent learners. And we are grateful to Michael Grinder, who revolutionized our thinking about student and teacher behaviors. Both of these voices have influenced us and are infused throughout our work with children and teachers and our writing.

The writing of our profession's experts has helped light the fires that continue to guide us and keep our inspirations fueled, especially the research and theories of Richard Allington, Michael Pressley, Ann McGill Franzen,

Peter Johnston, Emmett Betts, Lucy Calkins, Ralph Fletcher, Gerald Duffy, Marie Clay, Kelly Gallagher, Shelley Harwayne, Brenda Miller Power, Katie Wood Ray, Mary Howard, Donalyn Miller, John Medina, Ken Wesson, Doug Fisher, Linda Gambrell, Nancie Atwell, Clare Landrigan, and Tammy Mulligan.

Thanks to Lori Sabo and Allison Behne. They have heard much about this book from us before but always manage to find a set of fresh new eyes to read it yet again, providing feedback, helping us clarify our words and to think more deeply about students, teaching, and the Daily 5. They have a profound impact on our work.

To our friends at Stenhouse Publishers, who have become part of our family: Chandra Lowe, Jill Cooley, Rebecca Eaton, Chuck Lerch, Toby Gordon, Nate Butler, Chris Downey, Bill Varner, Zsofia McMullin, Lise Wood, Pam King, Jay Kilburn, Elaine Cyr, Erin Trainer, and Dan Tobin. Your encouragement and belief in our message, along with the constant support you provide all your writers, create the highest caliber of professional resources for teachers and students everywhere. And Martha Drury, your award-winning eye for design brings our book to life. For all of you, we are grateful.

An extra special thank-you to Philippa Stratton, our editor at Stenhouse. Your remarkable advice, guidance, and patience, along with your perfectly timed editing, has made this book better than we imagined. You truly are a gem and the heart and soul of Stenhouse. We are grateful to call you editor and friend.

We are so grateful for the love and support of our family. They help us live each day with joy no matter what we are doing. Doug, Dean, Jolie, Brad, Emily, and Madeline: Here's to the Majors.

And finally, we want to thank you, our readers, for joining us in supporting and creating independent and successful readers. We are honored to have our work be part of your library of professional books.

That Was Then, This Is Now: How the Daily 5 and CAFE Have Evolved

The typical teacher has children doing a lot of "stuff." How is what I am having children do creating readers and writers?

—Regie Routman

Since we first created and implemented the Daily 5 with our students in our own classrooms, and following the publication of our first book in 2006, we've had the opportunity to work with teachers all over the world. It's been thrilling, and deeply satisfying, to know that so many of you and your students have experienced success with the Daily 5. We have continued to work with children, learning from and with them, and as a result we have refined and enhanced the Daily 5. Whether you have been with us since the beginning or are just joining us, this new edition reflects our most current learning and the enhancements we have made to the Daily 5.

If you compare the table of contents of this new edition with the original book, you'll notice a lot of changes, in both content and organization. We've tried to make the whole process of getting started and sustaining work with the Daily 5 more accessible, and one of the appendixes consists of lesson plans for launching the Daily 5 and CAFE. (The CAFE system is our method for integrating assessment into daily reading and classroom instruction. CAFE is an acronym for Comprehension, Accuracy, Fluency, and Expanding vocabulary.) We've also included an index in this new edition to help you navigate the book.

Some of you may breathe a sigh of relief about one of the changes to the structure of the Daily 5: We no longer do all five rounds of Daily 5 each day, which confirms what many of you are already doing. This new edition delineates the difference between using Daily 5 with younger learners and older learners—in particular, those who possess more stamina than others. We outline how we typically settle into three rounds of the Daily 5 for those students who have less stamina and two rounds for those students who can maintain longer independent work times. We also describe how to manage both situations within the course of the day and week.

Whenever one starts the Daily 5, Read to Self is always the first of the five choices to be introduced. However, a significant change from the first edition is the order in which we now introduce the other Daily 5 choices. We no longer introduce Read to Someone as our second choice. Instead, we introduce Work on Writing as the second Daily 5 and introduce the other choices in whichever order seems most appropriate for the particular group of children who are with us. But how does one know when it is time to introduce the other Daily 5 choices? How do we prepare our students for the launch of each new Daily 5 choice? Strategies for recognizing this timing and for paving the way to an easy launch of each part of the Daily 5 are discussed in Chapters 6 and 7.

In response to many queries from teachers, principals, and literacy leaders, we have included a new section on what is needed to begin the Daily 5 (and the Math Daily 3) in the classroom. We think everyone will be pleasantly surprised to see that little to no financial investment is required to change a classroom into a place where children flourish through choice and extended practice, all based on what research says makes the biggest difference in the success of readers and writers in the classroom.

In particular, we have paid close attention to current brain research and the implications it has on the length of lessons—whether when launching the Daily 5 or the Math Daily 3, teaching whole-group lessons or small-group lessons. You will read about how this brain research influenced our development and refinement of the 10 Steps to Teaching and Learning Independence (discussed in Chapter 3) and notice the central role that the 10 Steps to Teaching and Learning Independence play in Daily 5.

Even with the raised level of awareness that brain research has brought to our work with children, we have in our classes students whom we call "barometer children." Barometer children are those kids who dictate the weather in the classroom. We have a real passion for working with these students and have developed systems that support building their stamina at their own rate, even when it varies from the rate of the rest of the class. We have included many strategies for working with barometer students in this new edition.

Of course, what would a new edition be without including the new, simply elegant structure patterned after the Daily 5—the Math Daily 3! You will note that just like the Daily 5, the Math Daily 3 holds no content. It is a structure used to teach children to be independent during math time so that we can work with individuals and small groups. The Math Daily 3 is the configuration that holds the math block together, and we are delighted to share how it is used in our classrooms.

The Daily 5 and the Math Daily 3 are structures that we have designed, taught, and refined together. Whether sitting in one of our conference sessions or classes, or joining us for a cup of coffee, you'd be struck by how united we are in our passion and approach to learning, literacy, and math. So it was entirely natural for us to use the term "we" throughout this book, not because we teach together, but because the way we structure learning and work with children is identical. The use of "we" isn't meant to be confusing, but it is evidence that it wouldn't matter whom you were talking to or which of our classrooms you visited; you'd observe the same behaviors and hear the same language in both. We are sisters, after all!

And now we invite you to join us in our evolving journey with the Daily 5, taking it into your classroom and making it your own with your own students. We'd love to hear how it goes!

In the Beginning

■ ■ ■ ■ ■ When we were just starting out as teachers, we were acutely aware of the joys and challenges of our profession. We had students who devoured every chapter book they could get their hands on. Others struggled to lift a single word from the page. And because we live in a widely diverse community, our classrooms were peppered with students who were literate in other languages but brand new to English and life in the United States. State and district standards insisted that all students achieve proficiency, yet our knowledge was limited in terms of how to manage and instruct with this wide range of needs.

If you walked into our classrooms during literacy time in our first years of teaching, you might have seen children sitting at their desks, working quietly on assigned worksheets, or clustered at centers looking quite busy. Except for Jason. He was sharpening his pencil and bothering a group of students sitting nearby. At the same time, a group of six students sat in front of us ready for a reading lesson. We were working hard as we left the group and raced around to redirect Jason and help another student at centers. We headed back to sit with the group, but oops, there we went again, up and moving as we headed toward Katy, who was wandering aimlessly in the book area disturbing the other children trying to work near her. Katy said she was looking for a book. Our brows furrowed as we quickly tried to help her find one. We glanced back at the small group we had just left, who were no longer reading the section of the book we had asked them to read, but instead were showing one another how they could make their armpits squeak. We headed back in the direction of the small group, redirecting a couple of children along the way. Our reading time was this daily, frantic dance.

At the end of the day, we dismissed our children and then slumped wearily into the closest chair. We looked longingly at the beautiful weather outside, just calling to us for a long walk. But our eyes fell upon the stacks of "things" our children had done during literacy time. Those things ranged from worksheets that went with the mandated district reading program to projects designed to "extend" stories for the week: book covers, dioramas, and posters with main-character faces. All of these items, and many more, were used to keep children busy while we attempted, none too successfully, to work with a few small groups and individuals. Because we had asked our children to do those "things," we certainly had to look at each one and at least make a mark on the paper. For the hundredth time we asked ourselves, "But did those things just keep our kids busy, or were our kids engaged in literacy tasks that will make a difference in their literate lives?" We pulled ourselves to our feet and headed over to the dreaded pile of children's work. Along the way we were distracted by the disarray of two of the centers we had worked so hard to create the previous weekend. We stopped to tidy and restock them with the materials needed for the next day, already dreading the next weekend when we would need to spend so much time creating more centers for the kids to help keep them busy.

Much later, when we had finished going through the pile of "things," we glanced at the clock. We realized that our fatigue was growing and that we had not even begun to look at the children's assessments from the last week or the focus lesson for writer's workshop the next day. We had spent the majority of our time preparing for and reviewing the children's busywork. Our kids didn't seem to be making the growth we believed they were capable of in literacy.

Enter our rooms a few years later. There is a quiet and calm hum in the room. Some children are lying on the floor with book boxes full of "good-fit books" sitting next to them. As they read to themselves, a child nearby reads the pictures in a book, laughing out loud at a funny part. Another student takes notes from an interesting section in a *National Geographic*. Some children are curled up in a corner on pillows with partners, reading and discussing a particularly exciting section from the Delirium series. Two others are taking turns as they choral-read a poem from *Take Me Out of the Bathtub* (Katz 2001). Other students are scattered about at tables and on the floor, heads bent, pens moving methodically across the pages of their journals as they craft tantalizing tall tales, original song scores, or tearful retellings of a pet succumbing to old age at home the night before. Near the word collector, where our class shared vocabulary, high-frequency words, and word patterns, others are sitting on the floor or at a table, tongues between their lips as they focus intently on building some of the new vocabulary, word families, and sight words using a variety of simple materials. Others are writing some of their personal vocabulary and spelling words on whiteboards. Over at the computers, two students are wearing headphones to listen to reading, and on the couch a student holds an iPad and wears headphones, listening to a chapter book being read aloud.

Looking about the room, you may have to hunt a bit to find us. When you do, you will discover us deeply engaged with a small group of two or three students as we practice a comprehension strategy together, or immersed in modeling a new accuracy strategy in an individual conference. The days of leaving our small group or conference to manage children are behind us. We actually have our backs to the rest of the class—we're not even looking at them! Yet the rest of the students in the class are working by themselves, completely independent. Our intuitive sense of who needs to be redirected with a look or verbal reminder goes unused as the center of our attention is on the child or children in front of us. We are not distracted by someone approaching us with a question or to report about another student, because it rarely happens. The rest of the class, away from our small group or individual conference, continues working independently.

As children leave for the day, we chat briefly with each one. We easily recall a successful accomplishment each child had during the day. Sharing it with them brings a proud smile to each face and we follow this with a promise of "We'll miss you until you return tomorrow!"

As we turn from the door, we make a brief tour of the room, picking up a pen here and a wayward sticky note there. We stop at the computer to check our e-mail, return a phone call to a parent about next week's field trip, and make sure the chart rack has enough paper on it for the next day.

We then sit down and review the day's conferring and assessment notes in our online conferring notebook, CCPensieve (see www.ccpensieve.com). We notice that Allie has made progress with the strategy Check for Understanding and has developed some metacognitive awareness of its use. In our conference scheduled with Allie for the next day, we plan to reinforce this strategy and layer on another CAFE Menu comprehension strategy, Back Up and Reread. (These and the other reading strategies mentioned here are discussed in detail in *The CAFE Book* [Boushey and Moser 2009].) We take note of our running record with Edguardo. He is still having trouble with Chunk Letters and Sounds Together. We decide to work on that skill for the next few days with him and two other children who are having the same challenge. We review our notes on the progress of a guided group of three children who are all reading different books written by Rick Riordan and working on their comprehension goal from the CAFE Menu, using the strategy Ask Questions Throughout the Reading Process. We make a note to double-check with Ingrid as she works diligently on her vocabulary goal using a CAFE Menu strategy called Use Word Parts to Determine the Meaning of Words—prefixes, suffixes, origins, abbreviations.

About thirty-five minutes have passed since the children left the room. We look up from our work to check the time, glance toward the window, and notice the beautiful day outside. We scan the room one more time to be certain all is ready for tomorrow, grab our coats and keys, and head quickly to the door—still with enough daylight and enough energy for a long walk with the dog.

What Changed?

■ ■ ■ ■ ■ These are two different pictures of our lives as literacy teachers. The latter is the one you will continue to see described in this book. (Okay, so maybe it is not always sunny and beautiful dog-walking weather in Seattle; it is actually rarely sunny, so when the sun does shine we have to get out there and enjoy it!)

The difference is our integration of the routines and framework we've come to call the Daily 5. When building this learning structure in our classrooms, it was critical to demonstrate and focus our teaching on what the children and teacher are to do within each of the five components. It is this explicit teaching and practicing of behaviors that sets the Daily 5 apart from the other management systems we have tried over the years.

We never expected to create a new framework for our literacy block. We were frustrated with our inability to engage students in independent, meaningful reading practice that would also allow us to meet with individuals and small groups of children. We just wanted someone to tell us what worked and was most effective for students and teachers. As the answer eluded us, we were highly motivated to find the solution. We called upon some of our esteemed literacy colleagues—Margaret Mooney (1990), Regie Routman (2003, 2005), Richard Allington (2009, 2012), Lucy Calkins (2012), Nancie Atwell (1987), Steven Krashen (2004), Michael Pressley (2001), and Shelley Harwayne (1992, 2001), to name a few. We studied and read nearly everything each of these people had published; we talked to each other daily about our discoveries. We were like Scott, a first grader in our class who was obsessed with trains. He read everything there was about trains, every story he wrote was about trains, and he played with trains every other second of the day. We too were obsessed, and we were determined to find a more effective way to help children be independent with meaningful activities, allowing us to work uninterrupted with small groups and individuals. We agreed with Gaea Leinhardt, Naomi Zigmond, and William Cooley (1981), who found that the way teachers structure the learning environment and the way students spend their time influences the level of reading proficiency the students have attained by the end of the academic year.

We began to look more closely at how we were structuring the learning environment, and we developed a new plan for how students would spend their time working independently while we met with small groups or conferred with individual students.

We wanted to change the atmosphere in our classrooms, and our own roles. Instead of trying to "manage" students, rushing around the room putting out fires, we wanted to create routines and procedures that fostered independent literacy behaviors that were ingrained to the point of being habits. Our goal was for all students to have internalized these expectations and shared experiences in a way that allowed for every child to become engrossed in their reading and writing. Figure 1.1 shows how we changed our practices over the years to meet this goal.

We were no longer satisfied with drawing a clear line between our literacy curriculum and our management routines. Instead, we wanted to work within our classroom communities to create environments where reading, writing, and self-monitoring were closely tied together for each child. We had to trust that our students had the skills and desire, even at age five, to accept the challenge of making thoughtful choices during sustained independent work periods.

With our focus more clearly defined, our attention shifted to what the experts had to say about students being independent and the tasks that facilitated their independent learning.

Figure 1.1

Management: How We Have Evolved			
Management Element	Our First Years of Teaching	Ten Years Later	Now with Daily 5
Teaching and Learning New Behaviors	We mentioned behaviors once and expected students to know and do them.	We taught and practiced behaviors once or twice and expected students to know and do them.	We teach and practice skills until behaviors become habits and "default" behaviors.
Expectations About the Students	We thought students should come to us knowing the appropriate behaviors.	We thought most of the students should know the appropriate behaviors. If they didn't, we spent one or two lessons teaching them.	We know each class is different, and we spend at least twenty days building community, defining and practicing behaviors, building stamina, and assessing the needs of that particular group of children.
Monitoring Student Behavior	We monitored students' behavior by telling students whether they were doing a good job or not.	We began releasing to some students the ability to monitor their own behavior. We continued to monitor our most challenging students' behaviors.	All students self-monitor their behavior during the Daily 5. They reflect and set behavior goals at the end of each Daily 5 round.

Management: How We Have Evolved (continued)			
Whole-Group Management	We awarded class points for desired behaviors.	We praised children for behaviors we expected them to exhibit; one student was designated to record points awarded to the class.	The whole class practices, defines, and knows how to perform desired behaviors. No points needed or given.
Small-Group Management	We awarded table points and wrote them on the board.	One child was table leader and recorded the points we awarded on a chart at the table.	Groups of students practice and encourage each other on defined, desired behaviors. No points or tangible rewards are necessary.
Individual Management	We awarded individual "star cards" for desired behaviors.	Individuals recorded points when we said they had earned them.	Individuals self-reflect and confer with us about the particular behavior goals they are working to achieve.
Student Not Exhibiting Desired Behavior	We asked individuals to "flip a card" from green to yellow to red, and the card was displayed for the whole class to view. The individual stayed in for recess with head down.	We gave a check mark or made a note on a student's clipboard that only he or she saw. At three marks children stayed in for recess. Individuals stayed in for recess and sat quietly.	Student may practice desired behavior for a short amount of time at recess. This desired behavior may become an articulated goal this child chooses to work on.
Locus of Control	Students had an external locus of control. We gave rewards for behaviors children were expected to exhibit.	We started to teach students how to monitor some behaviors and the reasoning behind each behavior.	Students have an internal locus of control. Students have a sense of urgency with their time, learning, and behavior at school and hold one another responsible by encouraging and supporting one another.

Figure 1.1 *(continued)*

The Daily 5 Evolved

■ ■ ■ ■ ■ Our first encounter with the Daily 5 came when we were studying with Margaret Mooney, a literacy instruction expert from New Zealand. While she was explicitly modeling a guided reading lesson to a group of teachers, someone stopped the whole group and frantically said, "Margaret, I can't see how guided reading would work in my class. You see, I have thirty students. What are the rest of my kids doing while I'm trying to teach this small group of children?"

"Oh, you know," Margaret said. "They're reading, reading to each other, revisiting books, writing, and trying something new."

We quickly wrote these down, and we remember saying, "That seems too simple. What about centers, what about worksheets? How will we ever know students are learning if they don't hand in pages for us to correct? How can you ever get all of your students to do all those tasks independently?"

We consulted our colleagues' work again to see if they agreed with Margaret about these tasks. Was this really what we could have our students do while we worked with small groups or individuals? What did the research say about each task?

As we persevered, we found what many researchers already knew and had been saying for years. These were the tasks that made a difference in classrooms where students were achieving.

The list we first heard from Margaret evolved into the following five tasks, which continually surfaced in our investigation: read to yourself, read to someone, work on writing, listen to reading, and spelling/word study. The tasks were not enough in themselves, though. Children needed extended amounts of time to participate in these tasks. At the 2011 national conference for the International Reading Association, Richard Allington stated that children should spend a minimum of ninety minutes per day in high-success reading (98 percent accuracy, reading in phrases, with at least 90 percent comprehension), and any and all reading instruction should occur outside of those ninety minutes. Not only was this longer than our current scheduled literacy block, but we knew our students were going to need to build stamina and develop independence in order to successfully sustain the activities for that long.

What Sets the Daily 5 Apart?

■ ■ ■ ■ ■ Think about how you manage your literacy block right now. Are you using a basal, seatwork, centers, reader's/writer's workshops, or a combination of these? We have found ourselves using all four at one time or the other.

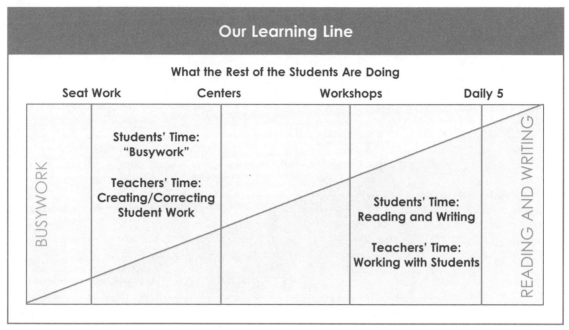

Figure 1.2

Looking back on our teaching practice, we see a definite progression in the way we have managed our literacy block (Figure 1.2). We began with a teacher-driven model that relied on busywork, workbooks, packets, and inauthentic reading and writing activities, which resulted in low student engagement. We progressed to centers, then to a workshop model, and finally to where we are now. The Daily 5 is designed to teach children to build their stamina and independence in each of the Daily 5 tasks so they can fully engage in meaningful, authentic reading and writing for an extended time. The Daily 5 tasks are steeped in choice, which increases motivation and student intellectual engagement. While they are engaged in this authentic reading and writing, we are then able to work with children, conducting individual conferences and working with small groups based on their needs as a result of our assessments. In *The CAFE Book* we address how and what we teach those individuals and small groups as well as the way in which we manage the assessments and their results. *The CAFE Book* also provides the organizational structure of our day-to-day teaching (Boushey and Moser 2009).

Many of us are familiar with basals, seatwork, and centers. They are structures we learned to use during our teacher preparation programs and in some locations are being used today. Many teachers have since ventured into reading and writing workshop, as we did. The Daily 5 is a workshop model. Actually, it is three workshops put together. What distinguishes the Daily 5 from other management systems is shown in Figure 1.3.

What Sets the Daily 5 Apart	
Students	**Teacher**
Engage in the acts of reading and writing for extended periods of time	Engages in the act of teaching students in many settings: one-on-one, small groups, whole groups
Receive explicit, focused instruction on building and maintaining independence and stamina	Explicitly teaches students how to build and maintain independence and stamina using the 10 Steps to Independence
Receive differentiated instruction to meet their individual needs through whole-group, small-group, and one-on-one conferring	• Delivers three whole-group focus lessons daily • Retains the option of teaching one to three small groups of children daily • Is accountable for conferring with nine to twelve individual students daily
Are accountable for staying on task, working on skills and strategies, and meeting with the teacher in small groups and one-on-one	Explicitly teaches the behaviors of staying on task through the 10 Steps to Independence and monitors accountability through one-on-one and small-group meetings
Receive explicit instruction on how to manage choice	Teaches students the purpose of choice, how to choose, and the behaviors that demonstrate a successful choice has been made
Choose what to read and write, where to read and write, and the order of reading and writing	Teaches students how to choose what to read and write, where to read and write, and the order of reading and writing

Figure 1.3

The first weeks of school for any teacher are about setting up the daily routines and building community. If you had asked us years ago what these first weeks of school looked like we would have said we started at the beginning of the basal and moved forward from there. In reflection, we realize we were blindly teaching curriculum without considering the individual and unique needs of the current students in our classroom.

Now we approach the beginning of the school year differently. Since the Daily 5 is an essential structural routine in our classrooms, the first weeks of school are dedicated to launching it, instilling literacy habits that allow for independent work. This time is also dedicated to administering diagnostic assessments that will inform and direct all of our instructional decisions.

Even if you begin the Daily 5 midyear, this book can serve as a launching guide. If you are frustrated because you are spending too much time trying to manage students and not enough time offering the most rigorous and joyful literacy experience possible, then the structure of the Daily 5 may be what you are looking for.

As professionals, we include an extensive amount in our literacy block. We teach specific reading strategies to increase comprehension, accuracy, fluency, and vocabulary. Reading instruction is delivered through shared reading, small-group meetings, one-on-one conferences, and modeled read-alouds. We provide opportunities for children to write, and we teach form, process, traits, and conventions. We teach students to be reflective and to self-monitor as well as to strive toward high national, state, and district standards. In addition, we assess our students both formally and informally, differentiate their instruction, and frequently monitor progress. How can we possibly do all of these things without losing important pieces, or for that matter, without losing our minds? The Daily 5 is the framework that gives structure to these components of comprehensive literacy. This framework helps us manage each piece of our literacy time simply and effectively.

An Overview of the Daily 5

When beginning the Daily 5, whether on the first day of school or midyear, we always begin by launching Read to Self (see Chapter 5). We use the 10 Steps to Independence (see Chapter 3) and start building Read-to-Self stamina, honoring the limited number of minutes our children are able to sustain reading and adding to these minutes of stamina daily. We always keep in mind the fact that starting back to school after a summer break means short stamina for all ages. It is typical to have stamina be as brief as two to three minutes, even with our older students. We want to set the bar high for expected behaviors, which often means we stop students much sooner than we may anticipate. Using the rule of thumb for the number of minutes of stamina our students have built before introducing the next Daily 5 (see the list on the first page of Chapter 7), we slowly add each of the Daily 5 choices so all five are introduced and stamina is built over the course of a few weeks. Once all five choices are introduced, there will be five short rounds of Daily 5 running each day, with students participating in each. Therefore, each of these choices will become a round of the Daily 5.

You will notice that we have included CAFE in the structure chart (Figure 1.4). This allows you to see the whole picture of our literacy block. The block begins with a whole-group focus lesson taken from our CAFE Menu. Students then move into their first Daily 5 choice. While they are independently participating in their choice, we are able to confer with individuals, meet with a small group, or conduct an individual assessment. Once children are no longer able to stay focused, or have broken stamina, we consider this to be the end of a "round" of Daily 5 and we gather the students back together. The pattern then repeats itself for the next four rounds.

Typically, eight to twelve weeks from the beginning of launching the Daily 5 we notice we are calling our children back for a focus lesson because time has run out rather than because off-task behaviors have shown us their stamina has run out. This is our indication that it is time to drop off one round of the Daily 5 in order to give children more uninterrupted time to read and write. At this point we commence having four rounds of Daily 5. The length of time for each round becomes longer, allowing for children to get into what Kelly Gallagher calls "the reading flow" (2009).

After dropping off one round of Daily 5, our students spend a few days participating in four rounds, with all five choices available to them. Again, once we see that we are interrupting a round due to time rather than stamina, we drop off yet another of the Daily 5 rounds.

The tables in Figures 1.5 and 1.6 show what our literacy block typically settles into once stamina has been built, eight to twelve weeks after the launch. As in Figure 1.4, Figure 1.5 shows Daily 5 for children who possess less stamina and therefore partake in three rounds of Daily 5. Many times we consider this to be a primary-grades schedule. That said, we have also worked in fifth- and sixth-grade classrooms that happen to have a group of students with limited stamina; these students also participate in three rounds of Daily 5 each day. We do not let age dictate the number of rounds in which our students participate. Instead, the number of rounds of Daily 5 is reflective of the amount of time students can maintain reading and writing independently.

For students who have greater reading and writing stamina—often but not always intermediate students—or for half-day kindergarten, two long rounds of Daily 5 are appropriate. Figure 1.6 represents a literacy block that includes two long rounds of Daily 5.

In Figures 1.4, 1.5, and 1.6, you will notice that Read to Self and Work on Writing are in bold. After students have built sufficient stamina with

Figure 1.4
Five Rounds of
the Daily 5

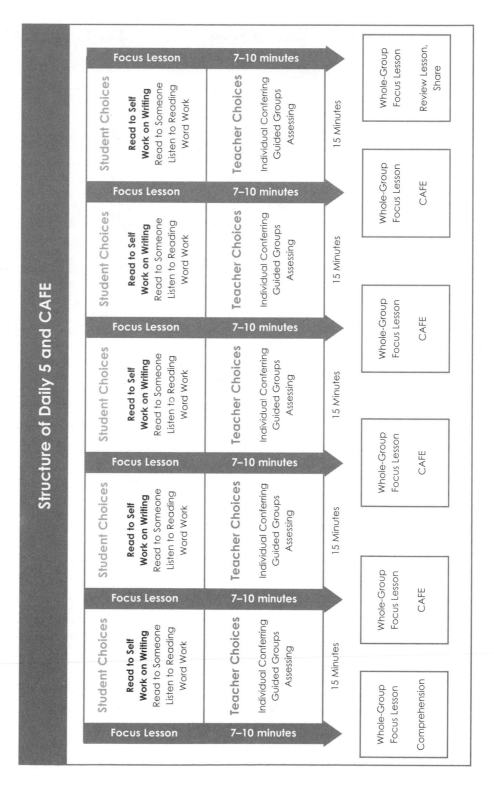

Structure of Daily 5 and CAFE

Round 1

Focus Lesson — 7–10 minutes

Student Choices
Read to Self
Work on Writing
Read to Someone
Listen to Reading
Word Work

Teacher Choices
Individual Conferring
Guided Groups
Assessing

15 Minutes

Whole-Group Focus Lesson
Comprehension

Round 2

Focus Lesson — 7–10 minutes

Student Choices
Read to Self
Work on Writing
Read to Someone
Listen to Reading
Word Work

Teacher Choices
Individual Conferring
Guided Groups
Assessing

15 Minutes

Whole-Group Focus Lesson
CAFE

Round 3

Focus Lesson — 7–10 minutes

Student Choices
Read to Self
Work on Writing
Read to Someone
Listen to Reading
Word Work

Teacher Choices
Individual Conferring
Guided Groups
Assessing

15 Minutes

Whole-Group Focus Lesson
CAFE

Round 4

Focus Lesson — 7–10 minutes

Student Choices
Read to Self
Work on Writing
Read to Someone
Listen to Reading
Word Work

Teacher Choices
Individual Conferring
Guided Groups
Assessing

15 Minutes

Whole-Group Focus Lesson
CAFE

Round 5

Focus Lesson — 7–10 minutes

Student Choices
Read to Self
Work on Writing
Read to Someone
Listen to Reading
Word Work

Teacher Choices
Individual Conferring
Guided Groups
Assessing

15 Minutes

Whole-Group Focus Lesson
Review Lesson, Share

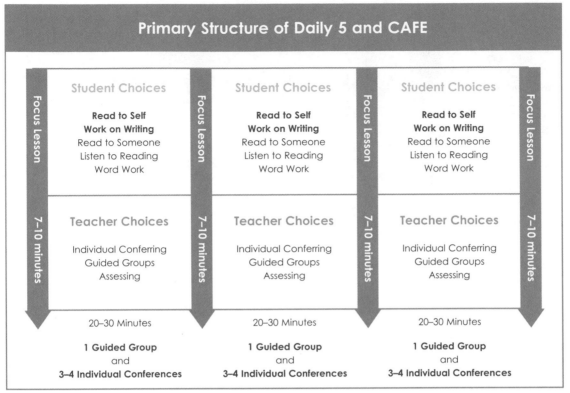

Figure 1.5
Three Rounds
of Daily 5

Read to Self so that a second Daily 5—Work on Writing—can be introduced, all students must select these two options each day during Daily 5. Even though these two are nonnegotiable, students enjoy the freedom to choose the order in which they will participate in each activity. The order students choose varies from day to day depending on their goals, motivation, and mood. Children select from the remaining Daily 5 tasks as time permits each day, knowing that by the end of the week they will have the opportunity to participate in all of the Daily 5 tasks, which helps meet their individual goals. Choice is one of the key reasons that students love the Daily 5, develop the habits of readers, and greatly improve their reading.

It may seem puzzling that students with more stamina are able to choose from all five tasks when they have only two rounds of Daily 5—with one round being Read to Self and the other Work on Writing. What we have learned is that students who have longer amounts of stamina are often those who are more advanced readers. Once students read at the third- to fourth-grade level or higher, they become "in-the-head" readers and prefer Read to Self, eliminating their need for Read to Someone. Typically students who take part in Read to Someone are our younger stu-

Figure 1.6
Two Rounds of
Daily 5

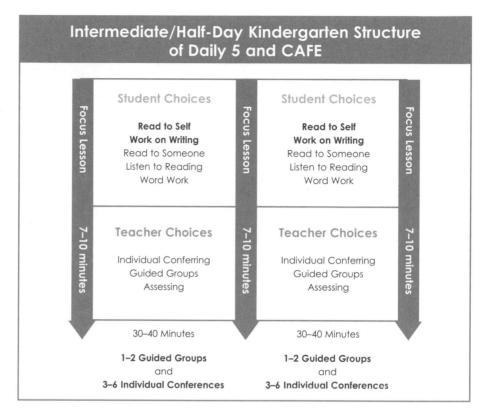

Figure 1.6
Two Rounds of
Daily 5

dents or students who are high auditory, meaning they need to read aloud to comprehend. Those students who participate in only two rounds typically do Read to Self and Work on Writing in any order. However, there are always exceptions. Meeting the needs of each individual student, we guide those who need Listen to Reading, Read to Someone, or Word Work to choose those as well over the course of the week.

Likewise we often have students who are not in need of Listen to Reading outside of our daily picture and chapter book read-alouds. The exception comes with our children who are non-English or beginning English speakers. Since we rarely acquire reading materials for the many different first languages of our diverse English Language Learning students, immersing them in English through Listen to Reading is an effective use of their time. Therefore, each day our students must choose some type of reading—Read to Self, Read to Someone, or Listen to Reading—for their Read-to-Self time (as indicated in bold type in Figures 1.5 and 1.6).

If our students who take part in the two rounds of Daily 5 need to have Word Work as a choice (not all do) they check in with Work on Writing and then, using a stopwatch or clock, time themselves for ten minutes of

Word Work. Then they quietly put away their materials and move right into Work on Writing.

The bottom line is, the Daily 5 is not a prescriptive program to be followed blindly, the same way each day, month, and year. Instead, we as educators need to respond and react to the diverse needs of our own students.

How Daily 5 and CAFE Fit Together

■ ■ ■ ■ ■ Figures 1.4, 1.5, and 1.6 are visual models of how Daily 5 and CAFE work together. Our whole-group instruction takes place with strategies from our CAFE Menu, and each round of Daily 5 allows students choices about which tasks to participate in (teachers have instructional choices as well!). Figure 1.5 represents a full literacy block, where a class spends 90–120 minutes engaged in literacy. The teacher starts the literacy block with a whole-group focus lesson, as indicated by the first blue band. After the short, whole-group focus lesson, the students choose and independently engage in one of the Daily 5 tasks for the whole round, as noted in the first top square. At the same time, the teacher chooses to work with small groups of students, confers one-on-one, and/or assesses students, as shown in the bottom square. When students reach the end of their stamina (as you'll see throughout this book, we often refer to this as "breaking stamina"), the teacher rings the chime and pulls all the students back together for a whole-group focus lesson, shown in Figure 1.5 by the second blue band.

In Figures 1.4, 1.5, and 1.6, Daily 5 and its five tasks are represented in the top three boxes, labeled "Student Choices." CAFE is represented in the blue bands, labeled "Focus Lesson"; notice we have a focus lesson between each round of Daily 5.

These focus lessons come from our CAFE Menu (Boushey and Moser 2009). As the teachers, we decide the skill and strategy most of our children need and teach it during one of the focus lessons. The bottom boxes, labeled "Teacher Choices," represent another aspect of CAFE.

We created the Daily 5 to support this "Teacher Choices" part of our CAFE system. The Daily 5 provides productive work time to the students we aren't meeting with. Teachers instruct students in small groups or one-on-one and/or assess individual students while the rest of the class participates in Daily 5 tasks. Figure 1.5 shows that just as the Daily 5 offers choice for students, the CAFE system offers choice for the teacher. Daily 5 and CAFE working together becomes the perfect model to use for differentiating our instruction to best meet the needs of all students in our classrooms.

Figure 1.7

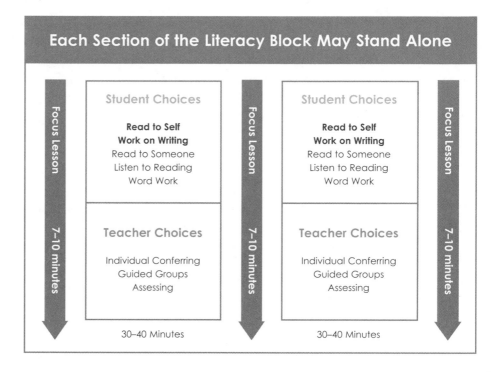

Because of our daily classroom schedules, many of us do not have a single, long block of time for literacy. One of the many strengths of Daily 5 is that once we have introduced all of the Daily 5 tasks and students have built independence, we no longer need an uninterrupted literacy block. If you happen to have one of those schedules that does not allow for an uninterrupted literacy block, as indicated in Figure 1.7, you can conduct the focus lesson at one time. Children can have a break in the schedule and then return to the class for the first round of Daily 5. The next focus lesson could be done before lunch, and the second round of Daily 5 could be held after lunch.

For example, sixth-grade teacher Mayte' teaches a whole-group focus lesson on the comprehension strategy Compare and Contrast (Boushey and Moser 2009) right before first recess. She ends this seven-to-ten-minute lesson by asking each of her students to make their Daily 5 choice before they go out to recess. When students return, they go right to their Daily 5 choice, and Mayte' begins teaching a small group, followed by one-on-one conferring. This round of Daily 5 lasts about forty minutes. At the end of that time, her students report to band and orchestra. When they return, the class has fifteen minutes before lunch—just enough time for Mayte' to teach a writing focus lesson on developing leads. With five minutes to spare, the students make their second Daily 5 choice of the day before heading to lunch. When they return to class from lunch, the transition is again smooth and quick as the students move right in and start their chosen Daily 5 task. Mayte' circulates around the class, conferring with individuals. She ends this forty-minute round with a time to share and review the strategies she taught during the whole-group focus lesson.

The independence built by modeling and practice and the consistent structure of the focus lesson, check-in, and independent work time allows individual rounds of the Daily 5 to take place at any point during the day.

It is important to remember that the Daily 5 is simply a framework and does not hold any curriculum content. It is about creating instructional routines with students through focused teaching, student modeling, and practice. Daily 5 also helps students build stamina, develop independence, and make successful choices. Once the Daily 5 has become a habit for children, we use our students' individual assessment results, our CAFE Menu (Boushey and Moser 2009), and our district, state, and national resources to present daily focus lessons and teach students individually and in small groups, meeting the instructional needs and goals for each child in our care.

Our Core Beliefs: The Foundations of the Daily 5

Respected adults engage in respect-full interactions in which respectful students can bloom.

—Marie-Nathalie Beaudoin

What beliefs and principles influence your teaching and learning goals? As we work to create independent learners, the following core beliefs serve as the foundation upon which the Daily 5 is built.

- Trust and Respect
- Community
- Choice
- Accountability
- Brain Research
- Transitions as Brain and Body Breaks
- 10 Steps to Independence

In this chapter we describe the first six beliefs listed here. Chapter 3 is dedicated to the seventh, the 10 Steps to Independence.

Trust and Respect

Meaningful learning requires respect and trust between the teacher and students. Taking time to build trust and demonstrate respect is the foundation upon which all other elements of learning are built. Each child is worthy of trust and respect.

Prior to developing the Daily 5, we underestimated our students' abilities to read or write for an extended period of time on their own. Because we didn't believe our students capable of doing it, we didn't trust them to do it. And with little respect for our students' abilities to sustain independent reading and writing, we thought they needed to have "activities" to keep them busy. After all, reading for an extended period of time was foreign to them, but activities were certainly not new.

The change came when we realized that the reason our students were unable to stay engaged was the fact that we were asking them to do unauthentic activities and had never explicitly taught them how to engage in meaningful reading and writing. Looking back, it seems odd to us. If children came to our class needing to be taught to become better readers, we had such respect for them; of course we would teach them the skills and strategies to achieve that goal. However, if students came to our class without the stamina or engagement skills needed to sustain reading and writing, we didn't realize we should teach them these things just as we taught reading skills and strategies to them. We simply assumed we couldn't trust them to read and write independently, so we put "activities" into their hands in an effort to keep them independently engaged. We finally realized that we could *teach* students how to build stamina and stay engaged in reading and writing for longer periods of time.

The Daily 5 works when we trust students, but it is not a blind trust. Through the 10 Steps to Independence (see Chapter 3) and guided practice, behaviors that can be sustained over time are gradually developed. Because we have taught our students how to read and write independently, we now trust and respect their abilities and can focus on teaching rather than policing. Individual students manage their own behavior. Children rise or fall, according to our expectations.

Trusting children is the underpinning of what makes the Daily 5 work. Trust is believing the best of others, even if actions or behaviors seem incongruent. If, while reading a book that is both a good fit and interesting, a student doesn't read the whole time, trust allows us to believe that the student hasn't yet developed stamina. When explicit instruction and extended practice are combined, our students acquire the skills necessary to become trusted, independent learners.

At times, despite having learned and practiced the skills of being independent learners, some students' stamina may falter or they may find themselves not being independent. Our deep-rooted trust in children's ability to learn the necessary skills of independence through explicit instruction and guided practice is what allows us to teach them again and trust them again. We look at these children and say to ourselves, "They are not being mischievous or malevolent; they need more instructional support and time to build stamina."

When Maria and Isaiah were in our class they were often the students who ran out of stamina first. Even well into the year they had physiological challenges that made it difficult to maintain stamina on some days. Every day, as the whole-group focus lesson concluded, we dismissed the rest of the students and then privately touched base with Maria and Isaiah and asked them to tell us what their plan was and double-checked that they knew what to do. On the days when their stamina was tapped out well before the other students' stamina, we would kindly bring the two of them back together, do another check-in with them, repeating instruction and practice if necessary, and then trust that they knew what to do and would carry it out.

Sometimes Maria and Isaiah were able to participate in all three rounds of Daily 5 with no extra support. Other days they needed us to have patience and guide them by making certain they knew what to do.

Even on difficult days, the key was to trust Maria and Isaiah. Knowing they were doing the best they were able to do and giving them more support, we sent the clear message, "Even though you just lost stamina early, we don't carry the memory of that off-task behavior into the next round. We believe in you. We trust that you can do it."

Community

■ ■ ■ ■ ■ We spend a great deal of effort creating and maintaining a healthy classroom culture. We build from a foundation of trust and respect to create an environment of learning and caring for all students. It starts with getting to know each other the first days of school and is embedded in the schedules we design together, the rules we construct together, the writing we fashion as a group, and the stories we read and draw on. The environment of the community becomes more intricate with each shared activity and lesson. For example, for weeks after reading aloud *The False Prince* by Jennifer A. Nielsen, it wasn't unusual to hear the class talking about Sage, the lead character. Each new group of children will fashion their own unique community based on the schema they bring to the classroom. This, our shared experiences and knowledge, binds us together.

A sense of community empowers students to hold others accountable for behaviors, learning, respect, and kindness. If a student is disruptive during work time, the community will join together to encourage, support, and positively hold this child accountable for his or her learning behavior, often referring to one of the posted I-charts to do so (see "I-charts," page 60). For example, when Michelle had a difficult time staying focused on her book, Talon quietly and respectfully redirected her by referring to the I-chart for Read-to-Self behaviors.

We work hard to help students understand that we are all in various stages of development. Students are taught to honor where they are and where their classmates are in their learning journeys. It isn't uncommon for two children to sit side by side, one with a chapter book and one with an early picture book, completely comfortable with the truth that each selection meets that individual's need at that particular moment.

Once the culture of honor and respect has been deeply established, the community becomes a place where achieved goals, and even small steps of progress, are met with sincere rejoicing. It is group dynamics at its finest.

Michael was a new student to our classroom. He arrived with a chip on his shoulder as well as a report card and note from his last teacher indicating that he was reading substantially below grade level. And due to his attitude, Michael was at risk of not meeting the end-of-year standard.

When another student, Amanda, asked Michael to do Read to Someone with her, he was unwilling to read aloud, but listened to Amanda read to him. Each day she chose him as a reading partner, coaxing him to check for understanding with what she read, bringing him along into our positive community. After five days of Read to Someone with Amanda, Michael pulled out a good-fit book and quietly took a turn reading. This time Amanda checked for understanding. At the end of Daily 5 that day, as we were reviewing what we had learned, Amanda raised her hand and said, "I learned that Michael is a great Read-to-Someone partner and has really good fluency." His grin was instant, the whole class cheered, and Michael was well on his way to making the end-of-year standard, as he now felt the comfort of a community that honored all progress by each student.

Choice

Choice is highly motivating and it is one of the cornerstones of Daily 5. In an article on engagement in learning Gambrell wrote, "Choice has been identified as a powerful force that allows students to take ownership and responsibility for their learning. Studies indicate that motivation increases when students have opportunities to make choices about what they learn and when they believe they have some autonomy or control over their own learning" (2011, 175). In fact, not only does motivation increase, but also success: "It appears that students who are allowed to choose their own reading materials are more motivated to read, expend more effort, and gain better understanding of the text" (Guthrie, quoted in Gambrell 2011, 175).

Through Daily 5 students have control over what they read and write, where they sit, and the activity they participate in. Just as with trust, the opportunity to choose has to be earned and occurs only after instruction and practice.

Introducing choice in the Daily 5 can be daunting. Each year on the day we planned to introduce our students to choice in the Daily 5 (see page 110 for more on introducing choice), we felt a bit like we were jumping into the deep end of the pool without being able to swim. We would call each other and try to justify why our kids weren't ready to choose. But what were we really giving up? Control? A neat and tidy literacy time? Since we had taught our students to be independent with each of the Daily 5 tasks and had exposed them to all the different places to sit in the room through the lens of "Is this a place where you and others can be independent?" we would laugh and say to each other, "We have no reason to be nervous. After all, we've taught them how to be independent with each of the Daily 5 choices; the order they choose will not make a difference." What resulted, every year without fail, was a chorus of students expressing their excitement and oftentimes demonstrating extended stamina the very first day we allowed them to choose. We didn't need to feel anxious!

We recently met a new teacher at one of our conferences. She had taken over a very difficult fifth-grade classroom midyear. On her first day with this class, she introduced the Daily 5. All day she struggled with students' difficult attitudes and behaviors. She quickly got Read to Self and Work on Writing up and running so she could move into giving the children choice over their Daily 5 schedule. The day she introduced choice and had her students practice choosing between Read to Self and Work on Writing, all the students headed out to recess after Daily 5 time buzzing with excitement over being allowed to control their schedule. The most challenging child lingered behind. He approached this new teacher and in no uncertain terms told her she was "the coolest teacher" he had ever had because he didn't like people telling him what to do!

It rings true for all of us, not just the children we serve: When we have some say in the matter, we are much more motivated to complete the task.

Looking back on our literacy block development (see Figure 2.1), it is easy to see that at the beginning of our careers we maintained a high level

Figure 2.1
The Development of Our Literacy Block

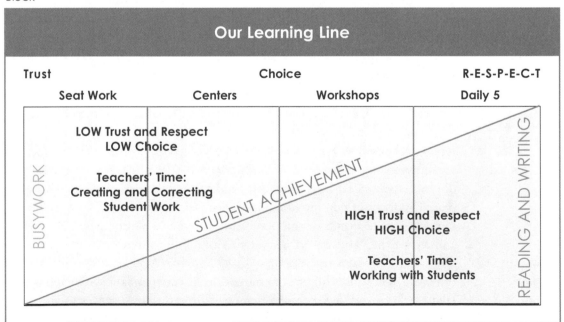

of control over our students. We were in charge of what they read, where they sat, and the activities they participated in. Early in our careers we had little trust and little respect for students, and we gave them little choice in their learning. As we look at our literacy block now, we can see that it was the Daily 5 that led us to a high degree of trust and respect for children as we have taught them to make their own choices.

Without a doubt, choice is an essential core belief and true foundation for the success of Daily 5.

Accountability

We used to believe that accountability was about us "holding" students accountable. Picture this: It was a silent room, children sitting at desks busy with the exact same worksheets and assignments. We were looming over students, clipboard or grade book in hand, keeping track of the completion of their work. Because many of the students did not have the ability to fill out the worksheets, we needed to be out among the children, managing and redirecting, flitting from child to child in order to help them complete their work. And since so many of our students were unable to sit at desks comfortably, this resulted in us managing their behavior. It was not a pretty picture. Our students weren't making the progress we knew they were capable of, so we began researching the components of a meaningful, successful, and productive literacy block. Our research led us to the five tasks that we developed into the Daily 5. We also realized that accountability is a two-way street. With the Daily 5, we needed to be accountable to our students by thoroughly teaching them what it looks like, feels like, and sounds like to participate in these productive tasks. Through the research and the changes we made to our literacy block, our perception of accountability changed as well.

Now we teach our children to be accountable for choosing their own comfortable spots all around the room where they engage in meaningful reading and writing for extended periods of time. When launching the Daily 5 using the 10 Steps to Independence, we introduce children to all of the spots they can work when we Place Students Around the Room (step 6). Over time, our children show they are accountable for finding their own work places by choosing a location where they can be independent and maintain stamina. During the work times, the room is not completely silent. Instead, we have taught students to be accountable for the level of noise they create, resulting in a hum of productive and engaged conversations. Students show their accountability by keeping their voices to a level that allows others in the room to work independently. There are always days throughout the year where seat placement and voice level are not up to standard. At that time, it may require stepping back as a class, having a discussion, or reteaching or reviewing the I-charts. If it is merely an individual who is not being accountable for his or her behavior, we may simply need an individual conference.

Children no longer require management from us to complete unrelated worksheets and assignments. Instead, we have taught our students to select meaningful reading materials and writing topics, which naturally results in a high level of motivation, engagement, and achievement (Gambrell 2011). Meaningful independence is the ultimate in student accountability.

Brain Research

If you're familiar with the first edition of *The Daily 5*, one of the first things you may notice when looking at the updated, linear look of the Daily 5 schedule (shown in Figures 1.4, 1.5, and 1.6) is the brevity of the whole-group focus lessons between rounds of Daily 5. The short length of time of these lessons is not accidental; it's a reflection of the importance of brain-compatible learning time.

Years ago we had the opportunity to hear Ken Wesson speak at a conference. He was the first person we encountered who made a direct connection between children's ages and the impact lesson length has on their ability to process and retain information presented during direct instruction. It was Wesson who originally taught us the rule of thumb that would change the results of our lessons: The average number of years our children are in age parallels the average number of minutes they can maintain attention during direct instruction—whole group, small group, or one-on-one—as measured by PET scans.

Our immediate response to Wesson's ideas was simply, how could he make this kind of a judgment without ever seeing us teach? We worked very hard to make our lessons from the basal as exciting and engaging as possible even though this sometimes involved turning on our inner actresses.

We clearly remember Wesson's lesson-length guideline rubbing us the wrong way, for at that time in our careers we were still using a basal program for our reading instruction. The basal program started with a whole-group lesson that typically ran thirty to forty-five minutes. You may be familiar with the lesson format: a warm-up that included a review from the day prior, then, of course, building background knowledge and introduction of vocabulary. By the time we would get into the meat of the lesson, twenty to twenty-five minutes had already passed.

Yet we did wonder if there might be something to Wesson's research. We had noticed that some of our fourth-grade students weren't understanding and applying the lesson's concepts as much as we would hope. It gave us much to think about, and, quite frankly, we left the conference with one goal in mind: We were going to see if Wesson's rule of thumb was relevant in our own classrooms.

We returned to our classrooms after the conference and promptly set up a video camera that would film our whole-group literacy lessons each day. At the end of the day we would rewind the lesson and watch our teaching. At first all we noticed was the delivery of the lesson itself: Did we hit the mark? How was the cadence? Was the lesson visual enough? Soon we realized that although we were caught up in reflecting on our teaching, which is not a bad thing, we were missing the whole point—to prove to Wesson that his rule of thumb didn't apply to us. We were sure our lessons were keeping our students engaged for much longer than the ten minutes that coincided with their age.

We turned the volume off so we could sharpen our focus on the children and their behaviors. Needless to say, we were never able to send Wesson a video to prove the research wrong. Not only that, but we noticed things about our students that we had never seen before! We kept an eye on the elapsed time on the camera. About seven to eight minutes into the lesson we became aware of some of the most horrific (or hysterical, depending on the way you wanted to look at it) "good-bye behavior" we had ever seen. Karima became hyperfocused on the pattern of the tread on her shoe, Ezechial used his fingers to separate the pile of the carpet and appeared to be counting the carpet loops per square inch, and don't even get us started on the fact that Jake turned completely around—yes, he had his back to us. Then Graehm actually got up and walked away! How had we missed all of these obvious signs that our children had reached their threshold for processing and retaining the information in the lesson? How had we not noticed when their brains were done?

Several books on brain research and brain-compatible learning have been published. In his book *Brain Rules*, John Medina discusses the fact that the brain has a stubborn timing pattern of ten (2009). After about ten minutes of direct instruction, the brain must make a slight shift in order to refocus. We simply cannot ignore the implications of these types of studies; if we do, we must know the ramifications of lessons that run over ten minutes—we are wasting our breath and our students' time, as the ability to retain the information is greatly decreased.

In a presentation at the Washington Organization of Reading Development Conference, Regie Routman spoke about the 80/20 concept. It used to be that 80 percent of our time was spent delivering direct instruction to our students and about 20 percent of the time was given to student practice of the concepts. Routman counters that if we want to be more effective with our instruction, we need to switch the ratio to 20/80. Twenty percent of our time should be spent teaching our children based on their immediate needs, as guided by individual assessments. Eighty percent of students' time must be spent on practicing the skills and concepts introduced during their instruction, using books and writing they choose. No longer can we afford to use the "spray and pray" method of instruction. You may be familiar with this: We spray our kids with general instruction from a program that is written without knowing each of our students' individual needs, and then we pray the instruction works!

Extended amounts of time for student practice is key. Our brother and his wife have four daughters, all high school athletes. As of the writing of this book, their high school team has just won its fifth straight Washington State Basketball Championship in a row, setting a new state record. These girls provide insight into the concept of 20/80 versus 80/20. They are not particularly tall girls, and quite frankly there are girls on the team who are not even all that athletic. Yet they beat opponents by thirty or forty—even by fifty—points each game. We had the opportunity to chat with the coach after one of the games. We asked him about this incredible run of success. He looked at us and said, "You are both teachers. You should know." Red in the face, we responded sheepishly and asked him to enlighten us. His response? "We play the game more than any of our opponents. We are on the court more, we get more playing time, we practice shooting more. Our conditioning is running up and down the court, not laps, lines, or sprints, and I am out there with them, giving them just-in-time coaching right when they need it."

His explanation of the dominance these girls have had on the basketball court for the past five years has been such an effective reminder of the power of practice. After all, if we want to get better at playing the piano, it certainly won't come from listening to our piano teacher talk to us about what to do for forty-five minutes and then practicing for fifteen minutes. Likewise, the more time we give our students to practice, with our expert, focused, just-in-time coaching available right when they need it, the better they will become at reading and writing.

This is why we have taken the research from Ken Wesson, John Medina, Regie Routman, and others and put it into practice in our own classrooms. Focus lessons are now exactly that: focused on what students need (no spray and pray method). Eighty percent of students' time is spent engaged in practice, and we, their coaches, provide just-in-time instruction. "It just may be that reading achievement is less about ability than it is about the opportunity to read" (Samuels and Farstrup 2011, 155). We agree.

A study by Anderson, Wilson, and Fielding (1988) looked at a group of middle-class, fifth-grade students and the amount of time spent reading every day. Looking at Figure 2.2, you can see that students who scored in the highest percentile read the most and had encountered the most words. Likewise, the lowest-performing students in the class not only read the very least but also encountered a minimal amount of words. Based on this research, Scientific Learning (2008) projected the effects if each child's average time spent reading increased by ten minutes daily.

As you can see, adding just ten more minutes to the reading time for the students in the highest percentile raised the amount of words they encountered by over 1 million words per year. As impressive as that is, notice the students performing at the twentieth percentile. Increasing their time spent reading by just ten minutes a day gave them an increase of 1,429 percent in word exposure.

Figure 2.2

How Much Students Read and How It Influences Achievement

Middle-Class Fifth Graders			Plus 10 Minutes per Day . . .		
Percentile	Minutes per Day	Words per Year	Minutes per Day	Words per Year	Percent Increase in Word Exposure
98	65.0	4,358,000	75.0	5,028,462	15%
90	21.1	1,823,000	31.1	2,686,981	47%
80	14.2	1,146,000	24.2	1,953,042	70%
70	9.6	622,000	19.6	1,269,917	104%
60	6.5	432,000	16.5	1,096,615	154%
50	4.6	282,000	14.6	895,043	217%
40	3.2	200,000	13.2	825,000	313%
30	1.8	106,00	11.8	694,889	556%
20	0.7	21,000	10.7	321,000	1,429%
10	0.1	8,000	10.1		
2	0.0	0	10.0		

Note: Adapted from Anderson, Wilson, and Fielding (1988).

Anderson, Wilson, and Fielding found that among all the ways children spent their time, reading books was the best predictor of several measures of reading achievement (1988).

Truthfully, we cannot afford *not* to have our students increase their reading time each day. And the brain research that encourages us to keep our focus lessons brief also enables us to provide our students with extended periods of reading time.

Transitions as Brain and Body Breaks

When we began using the workshop model in our classrooms, we soon realized that this structure was well aligned to what brain research was telling us. We taught a short focus lesson and followed this with an extended work session. The workshop structure allowed children the much-needed time to read and write and then share at the end. However, each day we struggled with keeping many of our students engaged during the work session. The extended time for practice was essential, but it just felt so long.

In the beginning of our workshop experience, we noticed that when our children's bodies were in need of a break from the work time, they would get up, get a drink, go to the bathroom, or bother others. We grappled with this situation, even resorting to giving them "things" to do—such as worksheets, activities, reading, and arts and crafts—to keep them engaged during the work time. But we realized that when their bodies and brains were provided with the needed break, our children were able to settle back in and continue with reading.

It was this realization that led us to divide the long work sessions into short work times separated by movement and short bursts of instruction. As a result, the Daily 5 contains two to five different "workshops" in a day. Each workshop, which we call a "round" of Daily 5, runs for the length of time our students have the stamina to maintain independence. Once we see our students' stamina for the work session waning, we stop the class and have students put away their materials and join us back in the class-gathering place. The simple acts of putting their things away and walking back to join together provide the physical break children's bodies and minds need. Once gathered together, we are able to provide more movement in the form of a poem, song, or chant, if necessary. A break in the practice session provides us with an opportunity to conduct a short, focused lesson based on the needs of the majority of the class.

At first we wondered if all the transitions would be disruptive for students or if we would have a hard time managing our students during all the movement. We have actually found the opposite to be true. The transitions allow for a longer and more focused literacy time, and practicing them also makes transitions throughout the whole day easier.

Transitions during Daily 5 provide a number of opportunities:

- A physical break from a student work session
- The kinesthetic movement children's brains and bodies require before continuing to work
- A brain break, which allows for refocusing
- A natural time to provide another short focus lesson

Many of you may be quaking in your shoes as you think of all the transitions that are at the core of Daily 5. Your experience with a class you have right now or one in your past may conjure up visions of noisy and wild behaviors during transitions and loss of precious work time. We also have had similar experiences in our careers, which is why we know that, as with everything we do in our classrooms, transitions must be taught.

We teach children how to make transitions, and how to build their stamina, by following the 10 Steps to Teaching and Learning Independence as described in Chapter 3. These 10 Steps are one of the things that set the Daily 5 apart from a traditional workshop model.

The core beliefs described in this chapter and the 10 Steps to Independence described in Chapter 3 are the groundwork for all of our work with children.

The 10 Steps to Teaching and Learning Independence

When we follow these routines day after day, our students can use their energy to grow as readers and learners rather than to figure out what we expect them to do. And we, in turn, can focus our energy on teaching, not managing, our independent readers.

—Kathy Collins

Our core beliefs create a strong base for student achievement. The 10 Steps to Teaching and Learning Independence are another crucial element of our core beliefs and the success of implementing Daily 5.

Early in our careers when we taught a behavior to our class, whether how to walk down the hall correctly or how to do Read to Someone independently, we assumed that once shown how to do something, children would do it successfully ever after. If we provided practice time, we often made the first few practices too long or did not repeat the practice sessions often enough to ensure success for all. Thanks to Michael Grinder's influence, we were able to realize why many of our students were not able to successfully demonstrate the behaviors we taught. Grinder explains that the brain receives input through three different memory systems: visual, auditory, and kinesthetic (1995). When information is stored in more than one of these systems, the memory is improved. Memory stored in the kinesthetic system evokes the longest-lasting memory. To activate this system, teachers can provide kinesthetic learning experiences so children hear and feel the behaviors expected of them. Over time, this movement is stored in muscle memory and becomes part of students' default behaviors.

Based on Grinder's research and our backgrounds and training in special education, we were able to, in essence, task-analyze the independent behaviors we were asking of students. This task analysis allowed us to formulate ten steps to improve muscle memory, build independence, and increase stamina. These 10 Steps to Teaching and Learning Independence are a unique and essential element that sets Daily 5 apart from the traditional workshop model as well as from other management systems:

Step 1. Identify What Is to Be Taught
Step 2. Set a Purpose and Create a Sense of Urgency
Step 3. Record Desired Behaviors on an I-Chart
Step 4. Model Most-Desirable Behaviors
Step 5. Model Least-Desirable Behaviors, Then Most-Desirable
Step 6. Place Students Around the Room
Step 7. Practice and Build Stamina
Step 8. Stay Out of the Way
Step 9. Use a Quiet Signal to Bring Students Back to the Gathering Space
Step 10. Conduct a Group Check-In; Ask, "How Did It Go?"

Step 1. Identify What Is to Be Taught

■ ■ ■ ■ ■ It may seem simple, but articulating exactly what is going to be taught is an important step to creating independent learners. Children and adults alike are better able to attend and focus when they know exactly what it is they will learn.

When identifying for the class what is to be taught as we launch each of the Daily 5 choices, we follow a simple pattern. This involves creating an I-chart (just like a T-chart, except that we make the T into an I, which stands for independence). This I-chart can be created on a piece of paper on the chart rack or easel or on an interactive whiteboard. Any medium will do so long as the chart is not erased; this chart will become an anchor to our learning and we will refer to it, add to it, and revise it all year long.

At the top of the I-chart we simply identify what is to be taught by writing the Daily 5 choice we are introducing (example: Read to Self). We add more text to the I-chart as described in the next two steps.

Step 2. Set a Purpose and Create a Sense of Urgency

■ ■ ■ ■ ■ Most of us have a deep need to know why we have to do something. Whether audibly or not, we often find ourselves asking, "What's in it for me?" For that reason we always clearly articulate and post why we do things in the classroom. Setting a purpose and creating a sense of urgency establishes a culture in which every moment of learning and practicing counts.

To create the sense of urgency with the I-chart, we follow the same pattern for the introduction of each of the Daily 5. At the top of the chart, on either side of the title, we record that the reasons we do Read to Self are that it is the best way to become a better reader and it is fun.

We'll never forget the time two administrators who were visiting our classroom experienced firsthand the sense of urgency our students felt working on the Daily 5. We were sitting on the floor with a small group of children. The rest of the class was scattered about the room independently working on their Daily 5 choices. The room had the lovely hum that is produced when children are comfortable, happy, and actively engaged in what they are doing. The two male administrators' deep voices resonated above the hum as they discussed their observations. Jenna, a fairly quiet child who uses her words sparingly, walked up to the men, tugged the pant leg of one, and said in no uncertain terms, "Mister, can you take it outside? You are too noisy. I am working on Read to Self. I really need to practice to be a better reader."

He glanced at her with a bemused expression on his face, held his hands up in front of him as if to say "I give!" and backed quietly out of the room. Jenna walked back to the corner of the couch she had previously occupied and continued reading.

Jenna felt the sense of urgency we want to instill in every child—the feeling that reading is so important, they can't and won't let anything get in the way.

Step 3. Record Desired Behaviors on an I-Chart

■ ■ ■ ■ ■ Recording on an I-chart behaviors that are most crucial to student success is the next of the 10 Steps to Independence.

When we wrote the first edition of *The Daily 5*, we suggested brainstorming with the class the most desirable behaviors when launching each of the Daily 5. We hope you will recognize that because of our ongoing learning, this is one of the many changes we have made to our Daily 5 system.

We found that when students brainstormed the most desirable behaviors for the I-chart, the length of the lesson became longer than recommended by the brain-compatible learning guidelines we had adopted (see "Brain Research," page 28). In particular, when young students brainstormed ideas, their list often contained a menagerie of extra suggestions for the I-chart, and the required conversations about each brainstormed idea simply took too much time.

Rather than have students brainstorm what it feels like, sounds like, and looks like to be independent as we used to do, we now merely record the desirable behaviors on the I-chart in front of the students and briefly explain each one. When introducing Read to Self, these are the five desirable behaviors we explain:

- Read the whole time
- Stay in one spot
- Get started right away
- Work quietly
- Build stamina

We'd like to draw your attention to the way in which these desired behaviors are written. Notice they are recorded in terms of the behavior we want to elicit from students. All too often it is easy to slip into the pattern of telling children what not to do: Don't walk around; don't talk to others. Michael Grinder found in his work with at-risk students that many children act upon what they hear at the end of a sentence or statement: walk around, talk to others. By subtly shifting our words to state the exact desired behaviors, children learn exactly what the behaviors look like, thus setting them up for success.

For young children with little stamina, we don't add all of the desired behaviors to the chart the first day. Instead, we name the first two desirable behaviors and write them directly on the I-chart. For example, on the first day of launching Read to Self, we write "Read the whole time" and "Stay in one spot" on the I-chart (see Figure 3.1). We add the other behaviors with each new practice session.

Figure 3.1 When introducing desired behaviors to younger students, we list and explain only the first two behaviors on the first day.

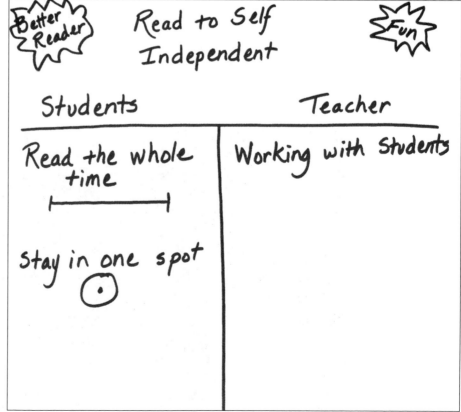

Older students, or students with previous experience in the Daily 5, may be able to draw from past experience and generate all desired behaviors or have enough sitting stamina for us to add all the desired behaviors to the I-chart on the first day. As with everything related to the Daily 5, we let the students who are present in front of us guide our teaching, based upon their experience, stamina, needs, and behaviors.

Step 4. Model Most-Desirable Behaviors

■ ■ ■ ■ ■ Modeling takes the two-dimensional recorded behaviors from the I-chart and presents them three-dimensionally, allowing the behaviors to come alive for many of our students.

Again Michael Grinder points out that the visual input of seeing correct behaviors modeled for the whole class and the kinesthetic input for those doing the modeling is the beginning of the process of creating children's muscle memories.

Modeling is a concept every teacher is familiar with, but often it may not receive the priority or time it deserves. Regardless of the skill being taught, we always have students model what it looks like when done properly.

We choose one or a few students at a time to model the behaviors listed on the I-chart correctly (see Figure 3.2). We stand next to the chart, direct-

Figure 3.2
A student models a desired behavior for Read to Self.

Photo courtesy of Gelfand-Piper Photography.

ing the class's attention toward the student or students who are modeling, and point out each of the behaviors listed on the "Students" side of the chart. We ask the class if they notice the modeler demonstrating the desired behavior. We then follow up with an imperative whole-group question related to the behaviors being modeled: "Boys and girls, if _____ continues to do these things, will he [or she] become a better reader [or writer]?" Of course the answer is yes!

Step 5. Model Least-Desirable Behaviors, Then Most-Desirable Behaviors Again

■ ■ ■ ■ ■ Step 5 is a powerful way to communicate expectations to children. Like step 4, it allows them the opportunity to see and feel, not just hear, the expectations. Even though it may feel counterintuitive to building independence, we ask a student in the class to come to the front of the group and model the I-chart behaviors the incorrect way—in other words, model the undesirable behaviors (see Figure 3.3). At times we invite a student who frequently exhibits off-task behaviors to model undesirable behaviors in front of the class. Since off-task behavior can at times be a call for attention, this strategy provides the attention desired by the student and allows us the opportunity to begin shaping his or her behaviors.

Figure 3.3
A student cheerfully models a behavior for Read to Self that is clearly undesirable!

Photo courtesy of Gelfand-Piper Photography.

As a student models undesirable behaviors (doing anything but what is on the I-chart), we once again draw the class's attention to the chart. We point out each item and ask the whole group if the modeler is showing the desired behaviors. (Of course not!) We then quickly follow up with this question: "Boys and girls, if _____ continues to do these things, will he [or she] become a better reader [or writer]?" (Again the answer is a resounding no!)

Next comes an essential component in beginning to redefine the students' muscle memory. After the student demonstrates the least-desirable behaviors and we remind students that those behaviors will never help them become better readers, we ask the student to flip into modeling the appropriate behaviors that are listed on the I-chart (see Figure 3.4). This step provides students the opportunity for their muscles to begin learning the correct actions of the behaviors, leading to a new normal for their muscle memory.

Figure 3.4
The same student models desirable behaviors after modeling undesirable behaviors.

Photo courtesy of Gelfand-Piper Photography.

Photo courtesy of Jon & Moch Photography.

Figure 3.5
The teacher draws the class's attention to the correct behaviors just modeled.

As soon as the student flips into modeling correctly, we refer to the I-chart again, pointing out all the correct behaviors being modeled (see Figure 3.5). Many students enjoy the positive attention, and they also show themselves and the class that their bodies are capable of performing the desirable behaviors.

We end step 5 by asking, "Class, if _____ continues to show these behaviors, will he [or she] become a better reader [or writer]?" The answer, of course, is yes!

Correct/incorrect/correct model interaction, originally taught to us by Michael Grinder, is typically done with all ages. The exception is for kindergartners at the beginning of their first school year. These young learners need time to find out what school is all about, and showing them incorrect behaviors can be confusing.

Through modeling, not only have we provided an opportunity for children to feel the correct behaviors as compared with the incorrect but also children have become confident in their ability to participate in the Daily 5 with appropriate behaviors. By making what's expected and what is unacceptable three-dimensional, students have a much clearer vision of what they are to do as well as what they should not be doing. The latter can often be even more important, because it clarifies and further delineates the boundaries of acceptability within the classroom. When problems occur (and they will), gentle reminders affirm the students by letting them know they are capable.

After working with an autism specialist in our school, we learned that correct/incorrect/correct model interaction, as a three-dimensional representation of behaviors, is a highly effective way to communicate expectations for many children on the autism spectrum. It helps take away the notion, for example, of "I didn't know I wasn't supposed to put the book on my head."

Step 5 is integral when helping students of all ages learn to be independent.

Step 6. Place Students Around the Room

Once students have seen correct and incorrect models through step 5, it is time to transfer the three-dimensional look of the behaviors to each child by having them all practice within the classroom setting. Often observers in our room ask us how our children find places to work without being told—with no racing for spots and without using teacher-created charts to equally share what may be considered coveted spots, such as couches, rocking chairs, large floor pillows, the classroom loft, and so on. With step 6 we teach children to respectfully and independently choose areas to work in the room.

Beginning with the students sitting on the floor in the gathering space, we clearly communicate, "You are going to sit in different spots during the practice sessions for the next few days. This will help you learn which places you and others around you can work independently."

We then stand by the book box, or classroom library, area and quickly call over groups of five or six students. Each of the students in the first group picks up his or her book box—a container of some kind that holds students' good-fit books. Book boxes allow students to remain seated around the room and not have to break their stamina by getting up to find more books. We then point to an area of the room where he or she should sit during this practice session, again reiterating, "You sit in this spot this time. Think to yourself while sitting there, Is this a place where I and others can be successful?" Figure 3.6 shows students scattered around the classroom to work independently.

Often students who are either of a "that's not fair" mind-set or really want to sit at what they currently perceive as a coveted spot need a bit of

Figure 3.6
Students work
independently in
places
scattered
throughout the
classroom.

reassuring that all students will have the opportunity to sit in all work areas in the room so they can learn the best places for their success.

As soon as we've sent off the first five or six students to their work places, we continue calling students to the book box area in groups and place them swiftly around the room. Taking too long to place students can end in a chaotic disaster, as those first placed will run out of stamina prior to the placement of the last students. Therefore, we leave the children with the shortest stamina in the gathering place and call them last. Since stamina in the beginning of the year is short, directing groups of students quickly instead of one-on-one helps expedite the placement process.

Step 7. Practice and Build Stamina

Once students are placed around the room we step out of the way and allow them all to practice and build their stamina. You may remember that in the first edition of *The Daily 5* we had indicated that the first practice session should last three minutes. However, we never let a timer or clock manage children's practice time. We suggested three minutes simply to remind us that in the beginning we should anticipate that all practice sessions will be short. The first practice might in fact last only thirty seconds in kindergarten or as long as five minutes in grade four. We understand that, no matter how long or short the practice periods may be, when students exhaust their stamina it's an indication that they have given us all they can.

Richard, a colleague of ours who teaches seventh grade, told us about one wrong assumption he used to make every fall. He assumed that because his students were older, they would be able to start the first practice session with fifteen minutes or so. In reality, when coming back from summer vacation, all of us—students and teachers alike—struggle with shortened stamina! Richard found that his seventh-grade students often would have only four or five minutes of stamina during those first few practice sessions.

Building stamina looks different in each room every year. Some classes increase their stamina rapidly, whereas others may build their stamina by only ten to thirty seconds each day. We always let our students' behavior set the pace, and we remind ourselves that a new group of students will not necessarily build stamina like our previous class did.

Figure 3.7
We use this stamina chart to show students that their stamina grows with practice.

As our children practice, we keep track of how long their stamina lasted while exhibiting the most-desirable behaviors. We do this so that as a class we can chart stamina progress (see Figure 3.7, "Stamina Chart," which is also in Appendix A). This is an effective way to visually display the stamina growth and can help many students make sense of the concept of building stamina.

At this point it is important to note that step 7, which we've just described, and step 8, the topic of the next section, take place simultaneously.

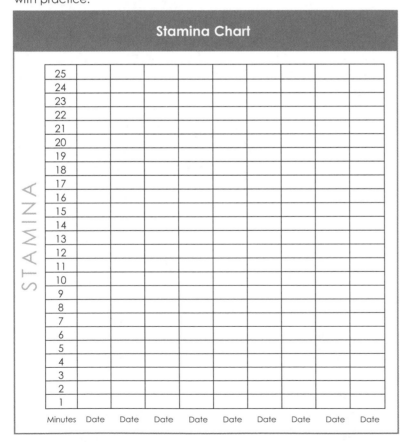

Step 8. Stay Out of the Way

■ ■ ■ ■ ■ Once children begin practicing, we stay out of the way until someone stops participating in any one of the charted expectations; this is what we refer to as reaching the end of their stamina, or breaking their stamina. Even though we stay out of the way, we surreptitiously watch for any sign that their stamina has been exhausted (Figure 3.8).

Many years ago, when we were first developing the Daily 5, we didn't stay out of the way as our children were practicing. We participated in the dance we thought all good teachers did: weaving around the room, whispering what a wonderful job they were doing as readers, praising them for staying focused, quietly applauding their on-task behavior. Our students built their stamina rapidly. However, the first time we attempted to assess an individual child while the rest of the students read to themselves, the class behavior fell apart. Children got up and walked around, went to the bathroom, got drinks, chatted with their friends, and came to us to ask what they should do next. We realized their on-task behavior had been anchored to us. We had unwittingly taught them to rely on our reinforcement and stimulus as extrinsic motivation to keep them on task. They were not the least bit independent. We had clearly missed the target of creating intrinsic, independent learners. It was a difficult lesson to learn but made a huge impact on our teaching.

During the launching period of each Daily 5 choice, as our students are practicing, we no longer move among the group. Instead, we quietly stay

Figure 3.8
Lori stays out of the way as students work on the Daily 5, but she keeps careful track of how students' stamina is holding up.

in one spot, not moving. Our stillness removes the external stimulus for children. This lack of movement from us allows children to focus on practicing the desired behaviors and attending to the task at hand rather than be distracted by us and rely on our constant positive reinforcement to help them build stamina. That said, even though we stay out of the way, we are aware of behaviors happening in the room.

It is important to note that staying out of the way takes place only during the launch period of each Daily 5. Once all of Daily 5 is up and running, we use the time that students are working independently to meet with individuals or small groups.

During this launch phase, as we stay out of the way, we are very aware of all that is going on in the room. This is the time we watch for the "barometer students," otherwise known as the children who dictate the "weather" of the classroom (see Figure 3.9). A barometer student will be the first person to run out of stamina.

Figure 3.9
The "barometer student" is the first student who runs out of stamina during the practice session.

Photo courtesy of Gelfand-Piper Photography.

Running out of stamina may be shown by a student getting a drink, talking to someone else, or looking around and starting to move toward us to ask or report something. As we stay out of the way, we listen and watch for the first sign of off-task behavior. Yet it is important to be aware during this time that we do not make direct eye contact or use our ever powerful "teacher eye." You know, the look that can put a child back on task from across the room. You may notice in your own classrooms that some students rely on being certain you are watching them, obtaining extrinsic motivation from nothing more than a look from the teacher. Avoiding direct eye contact during the launching phase is as important as physically staying out of the way so children can practice and build their stamina independently.

When watching for barometer children, it can be challenging to decipher whether a child has really reached the end of his or her stamina or is merely "resetting." To make the distinction, don't rush too quickly into stopping the class when a child looks as though he or she has run out of stamina. Dylan, a highly kinesthetic student in our room one year, was notorious for resetting himself. He would put down his book, stand up and stretch, look around, then settle back in with his reading, never bothering another student. He just needed to give his brain a break by resetting.

Staying out of the way while students practice assures that stamina for desirable behaviors is being built independently.

Step 9. Use a Quiet Signal to Bring Students Back to the Gathering Place

When we notice a child has exhausted his or her stamina, the remainder of the students often will follow suit. Therefore, as soon as one student shows through behavior that his or her stamina is gone, we make the quiet signal we've established in our rooms and say, "Please put your book boxes away and come join us in the gathering place." Even though it may seem unproductive, we stop children right away because we know they have used all the stamina they have. If we allow them to continue, inevitably we will move into managing the barometer children, defeating the purpose of learning to be independent. We also don't want students to practice incorrectly, as it is very difficult to change undesirable behaviors once they're ingrained.

The way we get children's attention can make or break the tone of a classroom. Since the interruption of a loud voice can easily trigger an escalation of the entire room's noise level, we use the power of a calm and respectful signal and teach children early on how to respond quickly when they hear it. In our classrooms, the signal is the ringing of a set of chimes. The balanced melody is different enough to grab the attention of our highly kinesthetic children, but not obtrusive enough to upset our auditory students. Other forms of a quiet signal may be the first few measures of quiet music playing, a gentle tone from an instrument such as a xylophone, or even a rain stick. (See "Chimes—The Quiet Signal" in Chapter 4.) We do not make any vocal or visual statement of approval or disapproval when we use the signal. We aren't judging the fact that students have worked as long as they can at this stage; we are simply signaling that we want the class to regroup so we can discuss our practice session.

On the way back to the gathering place after they hear the signal, all students put their book boxes away. Even though this takes time in the beginning of the year or launching phase, it helps students develop the good habit of cleaning up right away and will make transitions very smooth as the year progresses.

Step 10. Conduct a Group Check-In; Ask, "How Did It Go?"

Once students have joined us in the gathering space, we refer to the I-chart and ask students to reflect on their personal success with the behaviors listed.

Since our schools follow a standards-based grading system, we use a 1–4 check-in that we first saw used in Carlene Bickford's classroom in Waterville, Maine.

1. Below Standard
2. Approaching Standard
3. Meeting Standard
4. Exceeding Standard

For Read to Self, our invitation to reflect sounds something like this: "Class, put your hand in front of you as you think carefully about how you did today." Pointing to the first expectation, we say, "How did you do with Stay in One Spot?" The children put up the number of fingers that corresponds to the 1–4 check-in scale, indicating their perceived level of success (Figure 3.10).

We continue to review the expectations, one at a time, allowing students a brief moment to reflect and score themselves. "How did you do at

Figure 3.10
A student quietly holds up three fingers to indicate she feels she is meeting the standard for a Daily 5 behavior.

Photo courtesy of Gelfand-Piper Photography.

reading the whole time?" we ask. Then, "How did you do at getting started right away?" Based on their self-reflections of all the desired behaviors, students set a goal for the next practice. Sometimes we ask them to share their goal for the next round with an elbow buddy. Other times students share with the group, write their goals in a journal, or simply make an internal goal. For example, if a student was extremely quiet but did not read the whole time, she might set "read the whole time" as her goal. If a student read the whole time but could have done it with a quieter voice, he might establish "read quietly" as his focus for the next practice.

You may notice that auditory students—children who do a lot of talking out loud—along with the children who are extrinsically motivated, will want to give you a verbal check-in: "I did it, I was a 3!" We remind them this is their time to think about what they did well and what area they need to improve upon rather than sharing it out loud. We assure these students that when they indicate their standard with their fingers, we are able to see what they are thinking.

Our youngest students who are still in the egocentric stage of development will likely show four fingers for every behavior. Many times, students who are seeking attention will show a number of fingers that does not reflect their actual behavior. In both cases, we ignore the inaccurate numbers. If the attention seeker continues to be inaccurate in subsequent practice session check-ins, we may pull him or her aside quietly for a discussion. For our youngest learners, the inaccurate self-scoring may continue until they move out of egocentrism. We have found that, more often than not, if students don't get attention for it, the behavior extinguishes itself.

Once check-in is completed, teachers must make a decision about whether to move into another round of the Daily 5 right away. When working with very young students, we might decide that Daily 5 practice is done for the moment, and that we will revisit it again later. Older students may have enough stamina to whip through the 10 Steps again. Perhaps the class can add another behavior to the I-chart if necessary and complete another practice session in the hopes of increasing stamina.

Typically, we complete three to four practice sessions of Daily 5 each day during the first days of launching: once at the start of the day, then before recess, after lunch, and at the end of the day. Repeated practices the first days increase stamina more rapidly and solidify behaviors in students' muscle memory. The most important thing to remember is to tailor all decisions to the particular class you have in front of you; base your decisions on your students' individual needs, amount of stamina, and ability to focus.

Once independence is established and stamina is built, the purpose of check-in shifts from self-reflection to students articulating their individual goals and strategies as they choose their next Daily 5 activity. The time it takes for students to build stamina varies greatly depending on a number of factors, including whether they have used the Daily 5 in previous years and how much practice time they receive. We have found that getting Read to Self and Work on Writing up and running can take anywhere from five to ten days or more.

Reviewing the I-chart daily, modeling behaviors repeatedly, and gradually extending practice periods not only helps build student stamina but also establishes desired behaviors in students' muscle memory, ensuring they become each child's default Daily 5 behaviors.

What Do You Need to Begin the Daily 5?

Because believing that the dots will connect down the road will give you the confidence to follow your heart even when it leads you off the well-worn path.

—Steve Jobs

E ach fall the approach of the school year finds us creating our mental checklist and gathering materials needed to implement the Daily 5 in our classrooms. Preparing for Daily 5 is surprisingly simple. We find that few materials are necessary to support a successful launch.

Chimes—The Quiet Signal

The Daily 5 requires a number of transitions throughout the literacy block; this is one of the components that makes Daily 5 successful. In essence, the transitions break the literacy block into small, manageable chunks for students. These transitions take place based on the physical need for students to move. Michael Grinder's work, which we discuss in Chapter 3, helped us understand the need to save our voices for instruction rather than managing transitions. Instead of our voices, we use small chimes to indicate that a round of Daily 5 has ended and that students should rejoin us in the gathering place.

We spend time the very first day of school teaching children how to gather when they hear the chimes and then have them practice the exact behaviors we desire when we want their attention.

We are careful to explain the signal and its purpose. "Class, we want you to hear this sound [we ring the chimes]. We are going to use this sound all year when we want everyone's attention or we need to gather as a class."

If you find students aren't responding when you ring the chimes, you may need to refine the procedure. We use a strategy from Michael Grinder's book *ENVoY* called "Above, Pause, Whisper" (1995). Let's say it's the end of a Daily 5 round and we want to gather students. We ring the chimes to interrupt their work session with a sound *above*, or significantly different from, the background noise in the room. We then *pause*, not moving, talking, or ringing the chime again, long enough for even the kinesthetic children, who sometimes aren't tuned in to sounds, to look up. Finally, we drop our voices below the level of the chimes to a *whisper*, but loud enough for the children to hear us. This causes them to pay close attention in order to really hear what we are saying. In our low voice, we ask them to join us in the gathering place. Using "Above, Pause, Whisper" sounds like a subtle and perhaps insignificant change in the way we communicate to our class, but we are amazed each and every time at the results.

Sometimes this change in our approach to getting students' attention and drawing them to the gathering place works for all the kids but one or two. If this happens, we quietly have a chat with those individuals. Often

Figure 4.1
Lori rings a set of chimes to signal to children that it is time to put materials away and move to the gathering spot.

we find that they have a very specific reason for not joining the rest of the class. We work hard to listen and understand their reasons, which have ranged from "I'm not done with what I am doing" to plain old "I don't want to change yet." Depending on the child, they may just need a reminder that they can pick up where they left off during the next day's Daily 5. We also find that students who are very kinesthetic may take longer to come to the gathering place than others. They need to move about more; sometimes simply standing at the back of the group gathering will allow their kinesthetic needs to be met while they still listen and attend to the brief focus lesson.

Chart Rack or Interactive Whiteboard

The creation of desired-behavior I-charts as a class is an important component of Daily 5. (See page 60 for more information on I-charts.) Keep in

Figure 4.2
Daily 5 I-charts
are permanently
posted in a
highly visible
place, above
the CAFE Menu
bulletin board.

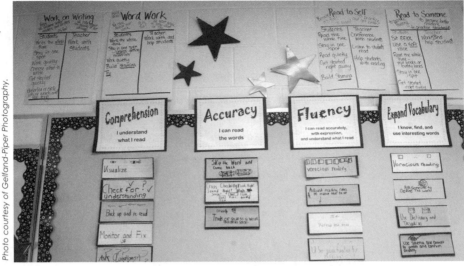

Photo courtesy of Gelfand-Piper Photography.

mind that I-charts will be kept all year as a reference to revisit when behaviors indicate a need for a refresher or when new students arrive (see Figure 4.2). Therefore, we find it imperative that I-charts be created on a permanent surface, such as a chart rack with paper, an interactive whiteboard, or even paper under a document camera.

Tools, Not Toys

Figure 4.3
A bin of tools can support stamina growth for "barometer students."

We never assume that all children will be able to build stamina at the same rate. Some students, whom we call barometer students (see page 48), will need extra support in the form of tools (not toys). Prior to the start of the school year we gather some tools to have on hand for students, just in case (see Figure 4.3). Those tools include sixty-second, ninety-second, and two-minute sand timers; small sandwich bags full of manipulatives, such as pattern blocks and Legos; stopwatches for older students; and alternative reading materials, such as I Spy books or world records books by Guinness.

As part of our preparation for supporting barometer students, we also think through the work spaces in the classroom. This often includes creating "offices" around the room by outlining large squares on the floor with masking tape or chalk, or by using square yards of fabric or moveable carpets. These offices support barometer children in finding a spot to sit and serve as a reminder to stay within the visual outline of that work space.

Book Boxes

■ ■ ■ ■ ■ To read independently, children need a variety of books at their direct disposal. In our classrooms, each child has a book box (Figure 4.4). A book box can be a magazine storage box, a zippered plastic bag, a plastic tub, or even a cereal box covered with Con-Tact paper. Each child has his or her own book box filled with three to ten good-fit books. Our beginning readers typically have eight to ten books, while our more advanced readers may have one novel and one or two picture books, a magazine, or even a newspaper.

At the beginning of each year, we usually do not know our children's favorite books, favorite authors, or reading levels. However, to begin teaching the independent behaviors of the Daily 5, children must have access to enough books to keep them engaged during this training period. Therefore, we spend a few minutes before the first day of school filling

Figure 4.4
Each child in our classrooms has his or her own book box filled with good-fit books.

Photo courtesy of Gelfand-Piper Photography.

each child's book box with a variety of books, depending on their age. If children come to school prior to the first day, you may want to have them choose books to fill their own boxes. Or, you could ask them to fill their book boxes as the first activity the first day of school. After we teach a lesson on good-fit books (see page 73), children begin to put their own book selections into their book boxes.

Jim Trelease (2001) says that children in classrooms with the most books consistently outperform their peers who are in classrooms with few books or no library. Allington and Cunningham (2007) suggest that primary-grade classrooms should have 700 to 750 titles and upper-grade classrooms should have about 400 titles. Our ultimate goal is to have 1,000 books in each classroom library. We have worked hard to reach this goal, using a variety of strategies to acquire an extensive library, about half fiction and half nonfiction. We have become fixtures at our public and school libraries. Both libraries allow us to check out forty picture books at a time and happily print out a copy of all the titles, which helps when it comes time to return the books. We begin each year with a letter to our families asking them to keep us in mind when they are cleaning out bookshelves at home (see Appendix H for one of our sample parent letters). We also ask families to keep their eyes open as they visit local thrift shops or garage sales. We let them know titles, authors, or series we are particularly interested in. Often, in lieu of treats, we ask our students to donate a book to the classroom library in honor of their birthdays.

Figure 4.5
This classroom boasts a large collection of books, supporting students' reading achievement.

In our school our goal is for all classrooms to achieve the large libraries suggested by Allington and Cunningham. When money becomes available in the school, we focus on adding to class libraries. We abide by the rule that "fair is not always equal." Teachers like us, who have been in the field for many years and have acquired large classroom libraries, take a back-seat to our new teachers who enter the profession with just a few books. We focus extra money and resources on classroom libraries that are just being built, as we want every child in our school, not just a choice few, to have access to an abundance of books. (See Figure 4.5.)

We are passionate about quality in addition to quantity of books in our libraries, so we weed out books that are badly worn, outdated, poorly written, or very commercial. This ensures that our classroom libraries stay current and relevant.

A Gathering Place and Focus Lessons

■ ■ ■ ■ ■ When creating a culture for learning and independence, two essential components must be in place—a gathering place and focus lessons.

A gathering place is an open space large enough for the whole class to gather while sitting on the floor (see Figure 4.6). The space also includes a chart rack and whiteboard or interactive whiteboard for focus lessons, class-created I-charts, an overhead projector or document camera, a CAFE

Figure 4.6
Students sit on
the floor for
lessons in the
gathering
space.

Photo courtesy of Jon & Moch Photography.

Menu board, and other teaching materials you find useful. We have a gathering place in every classroom in which we teach, regardless of our students' age levels.

Three of the biggest payoffs of a gathering space are behavior management through proximity, enhancing deeper thinking through accountable talk with partners, and the elimination of the convenient distractions kept inside desks. As they sit in proximity to each other, the teacher provides students with an opportunity to turn and talk, enhancing engagement and giving all students an opportunity to express their thinking. We are also more effectively able to listen in and join these student conversations, raising the level of engagement in lessons. When children sit on the floor together rather than at separate desks, they can better focus on the lesson and the group conversations about learning that are taking place.

Once students gather, the length in minutes of the brief focus lessons matches the age our students are in years, up to ten minutes. This aligns with the brain research done by Ken Wesson and John Medina (2010). The brevity of the lessons allows students' brains to engage and process information while we deliver direct, focused instruction. Keeping our whole-group focus lessons short and to the point results in better retention of the concepts being taught.

As discussed previously, we signal children to the gathering place between Daily 5 rounds when we see signs that they have begun to run out of stamina. This accomplishes two things for students at once; it provides time for a shift in their brain work and offers much-needed movement of their bodies—a brain and body break. As children join us in the gathering place on the floor, their activity and thinking shift from whatever Daily 5 choice they were just participating in to our focus lesson.

Students come to expect that between each round of Daily 5, they will not only have a much-needed time of movement for their bodies but will also receive short bursts of valuable and focused instruction. It is this consistent pattern that leads to the ebb and flow of teaching and practicing, teaching and practicing, that exemplifies the Daily 5.

I-Charts

While observing classrooms in New Zealand, we were intrigued by the practice of permanently displaying charts of collective class learning. If something was important, it was written down, and learning became anchored to the charts. Teachers and students referred to this visible learn-

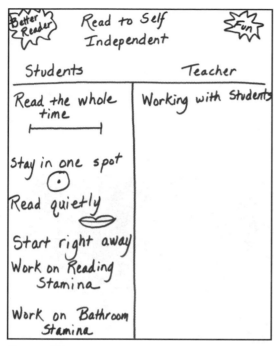

Figure 4.7
An I-Chart for
Read to Self

ing constantly. Disposing of it would have been throwing away a connection to prior thinking and learning. Now that we use these charts in our own classrooms, we've discovered that students can even remember where they were sitting at the time the charts were created. Making the charts constructs memories, schema, background knowledge, and experiences that become the multidimensional layers each student uses to create meaning and understanding in his or her educational life.

As each component of the Daily 5 is introduced, the class comes together to make an anchor chart, which we call an I-chart (I for independence). We discuss student and teacher behaviors to be exhibited for that Daily 5 task, and we record the results of our discussion on the charts. These I-charts are then posted in the room so the children's thoughts and learning can be referred to all year long. Figure 4.7 provides an example of an I-chart for Read to Self.

Classroom Design

■ ■ ■ ■ ■ Think about where you sit while reading for an extended period of time. Is it at the kitchen table, in bed, at an office desk, on the couch, or perhaps on the floor? Because comfort plays such a large role in stamina, we have abandoned the traditional model of a desk for every student, arranged in pods or rows. Instead, we now have tables and chairs for approximately half of our students to sit at one time, allowing for space in the room for a variety of other seating options. In the early weeks of school, students are guided to experience a variety of seating options to discover which ones fit best with their personalities and learning styles. With practice and guidance, our students eventually self-select places to sit that allow them and their classmates to be successful. Our classrooms typically have the following options:

- Low tables for floor sitting
- Regular tables with chairs

- High counters for standing
- Comfortable chairs or a couch or love seat
- Area rugs for sprawling
- A loft with seating above and below
- A few single seats in spots with privacy and reduced distractions

Figures 4.8 through 4.13 show how various classrooms have incorporated work spaces for Daily 5.

Figure 4.8
The extended table legs are removed from the table to accommodate students who want to sit on the floor or kneel while writing.

Figure 4.9
Children love to sit on the floor—leaning against a pillow or on an elbow—while the chair is home to the stuffed animals that are also reading.

Photo courtesy of Gelfand-Piper Photography.

Figure 4.10 Students discover the different areas in the classroom and use those areas to best meet their own needs for sustained independence.

Photo courtesy of Gelfand-Piper Photography.

Figure 4.11
This classroom feels spacious and cozy, and like a purposeful place to learn.

Figure 4.13
The gathering space is a place of learning.

Figure 4.12
A comfortable place for the body helps students read for long periods of time.

When launching Daily 5 we initially place children in different locations every day and always ask them to reflect on how that seating area worked for them and their independence. When children begin to show they are ready to self-select their seating choices, we remind them to choose the best place for their brains and bodies as well as for those around them. After all, some students will say that sitting right next to their very good friend is where they can be focused and independent. We continually guide the conversation to help students understand that their friend needs to be able to focus as well.

How do you know when your students are ready to choose their own spot? It doesn't always happen for all students at once. When it's time to send students to their independent work spaces around the room (see the 10 Steps of Independence in Chapter 3), many of them will begin saying things like, "I do really well if I sit over there" or "That's not a good spot for me to be independent." That's when we know they may be ready to choose on their own. Supporting children to make choices about where in the room they sit not only helps support stamina but also builds the culture of choice as well. Helping students focus on the importance of this small decision sends the message that they can be trusted to make decisions and choices on their own in this classroom.

Because whole-group instruction is always done in the gathering space, it doesn't take long to establish that the rest of the room is for important independent and small-group work, and a quiet rhythm and hum of purposeful work soon begins to develop.

Launching Read to Self—The First Daily 5

Just adding more time and space for independent reading is not enough. I'm advocating a carefully designed, structured reading program that includes demonstrating, teaching, guiding, monitoring, evaluating, and goal setting along with voluntary reading of books students choose . . . When an independent reading component is added, test scores go up.

—Regie Routman

Whether starting Daily 5 at the beginning of the year or midyear, we always launch Read to Self first. We begin with Read to Self because it embodies the language, routines, expectations, and behaviors on which all the other components of Daily 5 are based. It allows us to support students in the literacy block as they build stamina, and during this time we also teach the foundation lessons that will prepare students for subsequent components of the Daily 5.

Teaching children how to read on their own for extended periods of time each day creates the self-winding learner that we want in the center of our comprehensive literacy program. Students are actively engaged in the reading process when they have the stamina to read on their own.

Upon completion of kindergarten, five-year-old Ben was reflecting on his year. When asked what most helped him become a reader, he promptly replied, "Daily 5, 'cause when I do Read to Self I get more better at reading." We asked him to explain why Read to Self helped him become a better reader. He slowly cocked his head to the left, looked up at the ceiling, and began to speak in a deliberate, thoughtful manner. "Well, when I do Read to Self, I get to work on my accuracy. When I came to school, I couldn't read the words right, but I practiced every day during Daily 5 and now I can read."

Having children read to themselves is the first component of Daily 5 and the underpinning to creating independent readers and writers. On the surface, it seems basic, simple, and rather self-explanatory. However, we have found that in order for Read to Self to be a truly powerful tool for enhancing all literacy skills, it must be introduced with specific and focused instruction.

The key to successful implementation of Read to Self—and all components of Daily 5—is to start small and build in increments. When launching each component of the Daily 5, we use the 10 Steps to Independence (see Chapter 3) and the "gradual release of responsibility" model described by Pearson and Gallagher (1983).

Many of us believe in the value of gradual release, but when it comes to actual practice, we often make the mistake of thinking that if we taught students something and gave them an opportunity to practice it once or twice, they should be independent. You'll see that we are very conscious of the gradual release model as we introduce the Daily 5. We work with students to describe a new skill or behavior together, model it, practice it, talk about the skill again, and repeat the practice and discussion until the behavior becomes a habit. As you read our description of the first Daily 5, Read to Self, you will notice that each session includes multiple short practice sessions, with repetition and discussion throughout the first weeks of school. We have found that this repetition is key to successfully helping students develop good literacy habits, independence, and reading stamina.

The tone for the entire year is established during the early weeks of school. When we take our time during this critically important period, moving slowly and thoughtfully to build a solid foundation, it pays off all year long. We move slowly at first in order to move fast later on.

At this time, you may want to take a moment to explore the appendixes so you will know where to find details and example schedules that will help you visualize the process of launching the Daily 5.

The First Day

■ ■ ■ ■ ■ We spend our days prior to the new school year thinking through classroom design, anticipating the support barometer students might need, and getting materials ready for the launch of Daily 5.

If you looked into our classroom a few minutes before students arrived on the first day of school, you'd notice the walls were relatively bare, save for a few headings on our bulletin boards, including "Daily 5," "CAFE," and "Math Daily 3." The nearly bare walls await the documents of student learning—such as the Daily 5 and Math Daily 3 I-charts, class Word Collector, and CAFE strategies—that will slowly fill them over the year as the class moves through lessons and demonstrations and practice. There are books everywhere—not just in the library area but also in baskets and tubs throughout the room.

We write a letter to families before school starts, inviting them to bring their children to visit and drop off classroom supplies before the start of school. When families are able to visit us before the start of the school year, we show the children where to put their supplies in large holding bins, and give them a chance to browse books in the classroom library and fill their book boxes in preparation for the first day. These children know that their job when they come to the room on the first day of school will be to find a book to read from their book box and start reading. We also ask children who've visited before the first day to help classmates who weren't able to visit place their materials in the correct bins, from which we will pull the community supplies all year, and to invite these classmates to browse for books as well.

As the students come into the room the first day of school, we greet everyone, giving extra time to the families and children we haven't met yet.

Within minutes, there are children scattered across the room—on rugs, pillows, and at tables, happily browsing books or dumping crayons and paper into the bins we've labeled for supplies.

Three Ways to Read a Book

■ ■ ■ ■ ■ Once everyone has arrived, we pull the class together in the gathering place for their first read-aloud and lesson. We often start the year with picture books from one particular author, but any short picture book will do. As we do our first read-aloud, we teach our first foundation lesson to support Read to Self: Three Ways to Read a Book. We teach Three Ways to Read a Book to help the first practice of Read to Self go smoothly. In Chapter 6, we go into more detail about each of the foundation lessons. Three Ways to Read a Book is a powerful lesson for students who are not yet readers and for those who are new to English; these students are reassured that they all can read a book when we model the options of reading the pictures, reading the text, and retelling the story. Even though we have culturally diverse classrooms, usually most or all of our materials are written in English. Our ELL students who can read conventionally in their first language can actively participate in Read to Self too when we validate alternative ways of "reading." Teaching students that there are three ways to read a book eliminates students running out of stamina early with the reason, "But I *can't* read to myself; I don't know how to read!" Here are the three ways to read (see Figure 5.1):

- Read the pictures.
- Read the words.
- Retell the story.

We start with reading the pictures. This may be new thinking to our youngest or more inexperienced students who, until now, have believed that reading means the words or nothing at all. Many will say "I do that" after hearing us read the pictures. Much of learning to read, especially in the beginning stages, is a combination of reading the words, cross-checking with the pictures, and making meaning of the story. In this first lesson we also model reading the words. To keep the focus lesson to a reasonable length, we save retelling the story for the next lesson, which we present on day two or later the same day.

Figure 5.1
Marilyn works
with fourth
graders during
the first days of
school on Three
Ways to Read a
Book.

Photo courtesy of Jon & Moch Photography.

We start the lesson like this: "Class, we are going to learn two ways to read a book today. The first way is to read the pictures. Pictures often carry much of the meaning of what we read. I use pictures all the time. I use the pictures in this cookbook when I am trying a new recipe. Yesterday, I used the pictures on this page of directions when I was putting a fan together to cool off our house. I use the pictures in this book all the time to identify what kind of birds I see in our backyard. I'm going to read the pictures of a book to you now, and I want you to watch, listen, and see what you notice. Be ready to tell an elbow buddy one or two things you observed when I am finished."

We always use a picture book for this lesson, but we select one that will be of interest and appropriate for the grade level we teach. For instance, we might choose an emergent-level book with six to ten words per page for kindergartners, a Kevin Henkes book for primary-grades students, and a Patricia Polacco book for students in the intermediate grades. We tell the story by reading the pictures, stopping when appropriate to think aloud, predict, question, and so on. We keep in mind that, for now, it's okay if our words don't match the text or story, as long as the pictures support what we say.

"Boys and girls, you just watched us read the pictures," we say as we continue the lesson. "Turn and tell an elbow buddy what you noticed.

Make sure you both have a turn to share, and see if you can come up with at least two different things." After students have a chance to talk, we call on a few students, asking them to tell us what their partners said. This establishes a culture where it is absolutely expected that we listen carefully to one another and not just wait for our turn to talk.

"As I read the words this time, continue to be a detective and see what you notice." We read the text (or a portion of the text if it is a longer picture book) of the same story, again stopping periodically to think, wonder, and ponder over words, characters, storylines, and so on, modeling the reading and comprehension strategies that we will soon expect students to replicate. At the end of our reading we say, "Boys and girls, turn and tell your elbow buddy what you noticed. If you went first last time, let your partner go first this time. Be ready to share your partner's thinking with the rest of us."

Students notice, or we guide them to notice, that whether we are reading the words, the pictures, or a combination of both, thinking and engaging with the book continuously punctuate our reading. There is nothing passive about being a reader.

Later in the day or on day two, we begin a lesson by reviewing that we know two ways to read a book. "Please put a thumb in the air if you remember the two ways to read a book that we learned about yesterday," we say. Many thumbs go up. "Please turn and tell your elbow buddy one of the ways, and see if he or she can remember the other way.

"Great! I heard 'read the words' and 'read the pictures.' Now we are going to look at one last way to read a book, and that is retelling a story I've already read. This is the book I read to you before. Because I already read you the words and the pictures, it is still pretty fresh in my mind, so watch closely and I'll show you what it looks like and sounds like when you retell." We go through the book page by page, retelling the story as we go. "Did you notice that I used the pictures and what I remembered from reading the words to retell the story? It is a fun way to read a book, especially a favorite book! Today, while you are building your stamina during Read-to-Self time, you may choose to read the pictures, read the words, or retell a book you already read."

It is essential to teach what it looks and sounds like to read the pictures, read the words, and retell, regardless of the age and grade level. When children understand the three ways and the thinking that goes along with each, they will be able to practice effectively, becoming independent at reading for extended periods of time.

As we read the book—whether it be reading the pictures, reading the words, or retelling the story—we also pause periodically to model Check for Understanding, the first reading strategy from the CAFE Menu, which we teach each year with children of all ages and levels (Boushey and Moser 2009). We try very hard to keep the lesson length to seven to ten minutes, including the read-aloud, for Three Ways to Read a Book and Check for Understanding. Even after that short time, students begin to get restless, so it's time for a brain and body break. We have taught many different grade levels and know the brain research (see "Brain Research" in Chapter 2), so we know that the minutes students can attend to a lesson roughly match their age.

The first brain and body break can be as simple as having students stand up, turn to a neighbor, and share their name and one other piece of information about themselves. For young students we will often teach a song or a poem during a brain break—a great way to weave phonemic awareness into our day.

With book boxes filled and the first part of the Three Ways to Read a Book lesson under our belts, it is time to launch Read to Self.

At Last—We Launch Read to Self

Launching Read to Self involves going through the 10 Steps to Teaching Independence as described in Chapter 3. Appendix B gives an outline of this process for Read to Self. When we're working with older students, we may complete two rounds of the 10 Steps to Independence (i.e., two rounds of Read to Self), adding another student behavior to the I-chart and having another practice session, which includes trying out a new place to sit and adding on to their stamina.

When we work with younger students, we are typically done with launching Read to Self after one round, as their stamina is waning. For all ages, we will hold two to three more practice sessions throughout the first day, but for now we move on and begin teaching the foundation lessons for the other Daily 5 choices. (For an extensive sample schedule of lessons for the first fifteen days of Daily 5, see Appendix I.)

Integrating Foundation Lessons

Once Read to Self is introduced through the 10 Steps to Independence, the next burning question is, So what happens during the rest of the available literacy time on those first days, when students' stamina is limited? As mentioned previously, because the time involved in the process of starting Read to Self is driven by the amount of stamina our students have, the actual practice of reading to themselves uses only a small portion of the literacy time and builds slowly each day. The remainder of the literacy block allows for teaching the foundation lessons that students will need to learn before we can introduce the other Daily 5 choices.

We like to think of these foundation lessons as short bursts of instruction that preteach desired behaviors for all Daily 5 choices. This helps prevent the undesired behaviors that keep children from practicing correctly and building stamina. By teaching these lessons prior to the launch of each of the Daily 5 choices, we can jump right into the practice sessions for those other choices when their time comes. We want to avoid lengthy lessons at the launch of the other four Daily 5 choices. Since we have extra time in the early days, when the students are still building stamina, it makes sense to present all the foundation lessons then.

We developed foundation lessons for each component of the Daily 5. In the following sections of this chapter we describe the foundation lessons that we introduce during the launch of Read to Self. The remaining foundation lessons are described in detail in Chapter 6.

The Read-to-Self foundation lessons are the following:

- Three Ways to Read a Book (see page 68)
- I PICK Good-Fit Books
- Choose a Successful Spot (see page 88 in Chapter 6)

As you may have noted, with our youngest learners and in rooms with ELL students, we typically teach Three Ways to Read a Book before launching Read to Self on the first day. Teaching foundations lessons such as Three Ways to Read a Book prior to launching the corresponding Daily 5 is an important reminder of the reason for foundation lessons: to preempt behaviors that can stop students from being independent and building stamina.

Once the first practice session of Daily 5 is complete, and after a brain and body break, we choose one of the Read-to-Self foundation lessons to teach next. With older students in particular, we move into the I PICK Good-Fit Books lesson. This is an important lesson to teach during the first days of school, as older students need to be in charge of choosing their own books. After all, choice is a powerful force to enable students to take responsibility and ownership of their learning, which increases motivation and learning (Gambrell 2011).

I PICK Good-Fit Books

■ ■ ■ ■ ■ We have evidence from almost seventy years of research confirming that an independent-level book, or good-fit book, for children is one they can read with 99 percent accuracy (Betts 1946). Gambrell, Wilson, and Gantt (1981) said higher levels of oral reading error rate were linked to significant increases in off-task behavior. Given what the research and leaders in our field have discovered, we find it is essential to spend focused classroom time teaching our children to choose books that are a good fit for them, books they enjoy and that, as Routman says, "seem custom-made for the child" (2003, 93).

As classroom teachers, we understand the important role of good-fit books in the classroom. Our goal is to empower students to select good-fit books for themselves each time they go to the public library, local bookstore, or school and classroom libraries, without being reliant on leveled tubs, posted Lexile levels, or colored stickers.

The importance of independence in book selection was never clearer than when Pedro enrolled in Joan's classroom midyear. At that time, it was popular to have classroom libraries set up with tubs of books organized by reading level. We did this, thinking it was a way of supporting our students and expediting the book-shopping process. After assessing Pedro, Joan showed him the tubs containing the books closest to his reading level so he could fill his book box and begin participating in Daily 5.

Pedro loved books and wanted nothing more than to be a good reader. At the time, there were no books in his home, but Joan was able to help him and his mom get bus passes and library cards to go to the beautiful public library. Joan will never forget the day that was scheduled to be their very first visit to the public library. The day drew to a close, and her parting words to Pedro contained phrases of anticipation and excitement for his very first library excursion that evening. She had already scheduled a special time the next day when he would bring in his library books so they could look at them together. Joan had a hard time sleeping that night. She was so excited for Pedro and could hardly wait to see him in the morning.

The next day Joan waited excitedly for Pedro to arrive at school. He had hardly walked through the door before she seemingly pounced on him and pummeled him with her questions: "How was the library?" "What was your favorite part?" "What section did you like the most?" "Which book is your favorite?" With eyes shining he told her all about the beautiful building and the fact that he had never seen so many books in his life. She eagerly sat down, ready to pore over his new books with him. But wait, where were his new library books? He quickly said, "Oh, I didn't *get* any books at the library; there were no red tubs for me to choose from!"

That moment with Pedro is one of those times in Joan's career that is indelibly ingrained in her mind. In an effort to support Pedro with finding good-fit books, she had actually shackled him! Her leveled tubs had taken away his power to find books on his own outside the walls of our school.

As we worked with students over the years, it became clear that there was more to choosing a good-fit book than simply picking a book from a leveled tub or merely reading most of the words correctly. We began to understand that a child's purpose for reading, interest in a topic, and ability to comprehend played as large a role in finding a good-fit book as readability did. Thus the birth of our "I-PICK" lesson.

Nearly daily throughout the school year we have conversations about good-fit books. We follow the I-PICK method consistently in our own classrooms and in the school library. The librarian, principal, and even school secretary know the method and use the language with students. It's a simple message with great implications and requires frequent conversation, support, and individual accountability to help make the learning stick. We teach children that one of the most important things to do to become a better reader is to read good-fit books, and the I-PICK acronym is just the tool to help them make great selections.

I PICK Good-Fit Books

I select a book and look it over, inside and out.

Purpose: Why might I want to read it?

Interest: Does it interest me?

Comprehend: Do I understand what I am reading?

Know: Do I know most of the words?

We teach children about choosing good-fit books by comparing book selection to shoe selection. Our opening lesson on finding good-fit books is an anchor lesson. As part of the lesson, we create an I-PICK chart that we refer to all year long. We come to school with a bag containing a selection of shoes: fancy party shoes, tennis shoes, snow boots, golf shoes, and our husband's much-too-large hiking boots.

I: We take the shoes out, one by one, and look them over, which leads to the next part.

P: We discuss the **purpose** of each shoe and the importance of wearing the right shoe for each purpose. We would not wear the party shoes bowling, and we certainly wouldn't wear the bowling shoes to a party. Then we relate the analogy to the possible purposes for choosing a book: to learn something, to escape, to build our schema, to be entertained, and so on. Each book we select must match our purpose for selecting it. Knowing our purpose is foundational to ensuring a good fit, in shoes and in books.

I: As we move to **interest**, we share that students wouldn't find soccer shoes or ballet shoes in our bag, because those shoes do not match our interests. They definitely match the interests of others, but since they don't match our interests, we do not invest our time or energy in wearing them. We discuss the interests that match the shoes we do have, and the conversation evolves, illuminating the importance of selecting books we are truly interested in. We then share how this relates to books we have all failed to finish due to lack of interest, as well as favorite genres, authors, and titles that we have stuck with.

With the current emphasis in professional literature on helping kids choose good-fit books, we had too often overlooked children's interest in books. Nationwide there is extensive focus on Lexile levels and readability levels, and oftentimes we forget that children, like adults, need to be interested in what they are reading. Interest is critical if we are to get students to read the volume of material that will help them move from being "survival" readers to lifelong readers who choose to read for knowledge and pleasure.

Before teaching the last two steps of choosing a good-fit book, we go back to our bag of shoes and pull out a very large pair of our husband's hiking boots. We look them over and mention that we want to hike and are interested in seeing the nature around us (so the first three criteria are met). However, when we put on the boots and proceed to plod around the room, someone points out, amid laughter, that they don't fit. Books that are too hard to read, or that we don't understand, are like shoes that don't fit. They trip us up, are hard to use, and not enjoyable at all!

Then we have a few students with very different-sized feet trade shoes. When the traded shoes don't fit, we can talk once again about the shoes meeting their needs of purpose and interest but not fitting: "Emily and Ben are both wearing sneakers, which are perfect for their purpose of going to the gym and their interest in getting exercise, but Emily needs a smaller shoe and Ben needs a bigger shoe. If they go to the gym like this, will they become better runners? No! If they go to the gym like this, will they have fun? No, so these are not a good fit. This is just like books! Books that are a good fit for Emily might not be a good fit for Ben . . . and that is okay! If they want to be better readers and have fun, they have to have books that are a good fit."

This is when we introduce the last two criteria:

C: In order to be a good fit, we have to **comprehend** what we read.

K: In order to be a good fit, we have to **know the words**. Since our standard is 99 percent accuracy, we do not rely on the old five-finger rule, where we would ask students to put up a finger for each word they came to that they didn't know. The five-finger rule is unreliable, because our first graders may have six words per page, and our sixth graders 300. We simply read a portion of any picture book, novel, or magazine to see if we can truly read almost every word. This highly successful accuracy rate leads to greater fluency and greater comprehension.

We model these last two components of I PICK with a variety of reading material: a picture book, a magazine, a cookbook, a chapter book, a medical journal, and a finance publication or technical manual. We briefly use I PICK to test the fit of each one, discovering with the medical journal and the finance publication or technical manual that we might be able to read accurately but not understand, or, in the case of the medical journal, may not be able to read accurately at all.

The beauty of the I-PICK lesson is that it is one of the key components to creating a spirit of honor and respect in our classrooms. Children feel free to select the books that will meet their needs and enable them to achieve their goals, and they learn to value and celebrate the choices their classmates make.

After we complete the lesson for the day, we spend time helping kids find books using the I-PICK strategy. We stay in the classroom if we have ample books, or head to the library if we don't, keeping an I-PICK chart visible for quick reference. Another option, which we have done at times, is to split the class in half, keeping one group in the classroom library to support their good-fit book selection using the I-PICK method, and sending the other half of the group to the school library where the librarian does the same. Many teachers are fortunate to have librarians who use the same language and reinforce the skill throughout the year when students come to browse.

Throughout the school year, when a child asks for help to find a good-fit book, we go through the very same process each and every time. Using the I-PICK chart as an anchor, we first ask them about their **purpose**. Is it to find a good story to read during the Daily 5, a book to help support a report they are doing, or a book to read just for fun?

Then we ask them what they are **interested** in. Would they like to see what else is available by a beloved author? Are they hooked on a certain genre? Is there a topic they would like to learn more about? Upon the completion of this conversation, we move into helping and teaching students how to locate books, then watch as they sample the text to see if the book fits the last two criteria—**comprehend** and **know** the words. Teaching a child to check for comprehension takes extensive guided practice, so we consistently check book choice with each child each time we meet in a one-on-one conference or in a small group. Some form of the I-PICK lesson is also taught weekly throughout the year.

Children who learn to select good-fit books are empowered to make excellent reading choices whether they are at school, at home, at the store, or in the public library. Having a variety of good-fit books available for all children is a vital piece to creating independence in the classroom. After all, hasn't every one of us experienced, at one time or another, the frustration of having students who spent the majority of the independent reading time looking for a book instead of reading? Not to mention the number of children they would take off-task with them as they were "shopping" for a book. Oftentimes our most at-risk readers or those who feel unsuccessful are the most skilled at "shopping" for books instead of participating in the act that we know will help them the most: reading the whole time. However, once children internalize the I-PICK process, they will no longer wander aimlessly, wasting precious reading time while looking for a book. Since we know that the very best way to grow as a reader is to spend lots of time reading, and that the majority of that time needs to be with a good-fit book, the I-PICK lesson, and subsequent reviews of the lesson, help to ensure that that is exactly what will happen.

The week we present the I-PICK lesson, we also send home a newsletter to families telling them about I PICK and asking for their help and support. We revisit I PICK in our newsletters at least once a month to keep it on the front burner for the kids as well as their caregivers.

As children grasp the concept of I PICK, we have them model their book selection process in front of the whole class. Seeing their peers choosing good-fit books over and over helps cement the idea for the rest of the class. We also invite guests (gym teacher, principal, parents, and so on) to share what their current good-fit books are.

We now have opened up the lines of communication for creating not only a classroom of children who are learning to choose good-fit books but also a room where all children are honored and respected for the types of books each needs to read to move toward the goal of being a better reader.

There are many variations on our I-PICK lesson with the shoes. We know teachers who have used different-sized hand weights to connect to good-fit books, "Goldilocks and the Three Bears," and even different foods! Choosing a good-fit book is truly a lifelong skill that even we use today.

One of the challenges we have when choosing a good-fit book is time. Think about the last time you went to the library or bookstore, or even looked for a book on Amazon online. The process of finding a book takes time. Children in our classrooms are no different. They need time to browse books in order to find a good fit. We remember a time when we would say to children, "You need to have a book. Just grab one—any one—get reading!" Or we might even say, "Here, just read these books." We are not proud of those times, as we know the power of finding a great, self-selected book. We certainly want to encourage children to take the needed time to find a good-fit book, but we also want to curtail our at-risk readers from the constant, daily reading avoidance of spending their precious Daily 5 time browsing for books.

We support children with time to find a good-fit book in a number of ways. Sometimes children enter the classroom before school starts—a great time for book shopping. Or we can dedicate the first few minutes of school to book shopping. Students can make selections independently or with our assistance, if necessary.

If we have a time to go to the school library each week, we often split our class in half, as we mentioned previously. We send half of our students to the school library, where the librarian helps them find books using I PICK. The other half of the class stays with us in the classroom, where we support them in finding books in our class library. The following week, we switch the groups. This allows our children to get to know the two libraries in smaller groups. It is very powerful when the librarian uses the same I-PICK language!

Each time we confer with students or meet with them in a small group, we talk about good-fit books. Individual conferences and small-group meetings are perfect times to make sure students have good-fit books as well as a wide range of books from fiction and nonfiction, since many of the small-group and one-on-one work will be done with the books they select. It rapidly becomes evident who is struggling to find books that they love and can engage with and that are not too difficult. Once those children bubble up, we make frequent appointments with them at the start of Daily 5 to help check their book boxes for good-fit books; we want them to be set up for success. When we check in with students frequently about their good-fit books, the process goes quickly.

Once children get the hang of how to use the I-PICK method to choose their books, they can make better use of their time shopping for a book.

Figure 5.2
Kelly Yahr
confers with a
student about
her good-fit
book.

Perhaps our favorite way to provide shopping time comes from Kelly Yahr, a first-grade teacher in Washington State (Figure 5.2).

Once a week during one round of Daily 5, Kelly's children can check in with "Shop for Books." They use that whole round to shop for books in the school library or classroom library (Figure 5.3). Providing this time honors students who are unable to come before school, honors the various times students are ready to swap books out, and provides a way for reluctant readers to shop for books without using it as an avoidance technique. Using our Daily 5 Check-In form (explained in Chapter 7), we are able to jot down each child's Daily 5 choices each week, so if they try checking in with Shop for Books and have already done so, we can gently nudge them to make another choice. Kelly's structure also provides an extended period of time to look for books. It takes time to peruse, browse, and try out books to see if we like them.

Figure 5.3
A student
carefully looks
through a bin of
books in the
classroom library
during her book-
shopping time.

We think it is important to remember that choosing a good-fit book is a necessary part of being a reader. We have found that if behavior seems to be a bit bumpy during the Daily 5, the problem often lies with the student's book selection. We check to see if perhaps books need to be changed or whether a student needs our help to find a book or series of books they really love so they can get into what Kelly Gallagher calls "the reading flow" (2009).

By the time we've presented the first I-PICK lesson and students have had time to try out the process, it may only be midmorning on the first day of school, but already a lot of hard work has been accomplished. With students needing to move, we take time for another brain break to tour the school and start teaching the hallway behaviors. We set up an I-chart by the door labeled "Walking in the Hall." While everyone stands by the door we quickly list a few desirable hallway behaviors—keep your hands to yourself, walk quietly to respect other classes' learning, and, one of our favorites with young children, "hips and lips." Hands on hips. Lips closed. It's a trick that makes the class quiet and respectful hallway walkers.

Adding the Other Foundation Lessons

■ ■ ■ ■ ■ After the class returns from the school tour, we take a quick look at the other foundation lessons on our list. We know we will work our way through the whole list of foundation lessons in the first week or so, and our students will become progressively more independent each day. Since morning has been filled with lots of reading, it's time to do some writing with a lesson from the Work on Writing portion of foundation lessons.

Work-on-Writing Foundation Lessons
- Underline Words You Don't Know How to Spell, and Move On
- Set Up a Notebook
- Choose What to Write About

We know that one of the first components that can interrupt a student writer's stamina is the dreaded, "Can you tell me how to spell . . . ?" Reluctant writers, in particular, are masterful at finding ways to avoid writing, and this is a classic trick.

After we bring the class together in the gathering place, we begin a modeled writing lesson. In our classrooms we have found that one of the best things we can do for our students' writing is to write in front of them each day. As we write, we think aloud for our students so they can see what happens in a writer's head. We model writing about something in our lives. It is important to write about things that our students can relate to: playing on the playground, taking a walk with the dog, what we ate for dinner last night, and so on. As we write and think aloud we model underlining words and moving on when we come to a word we aren't quite sure how to spell. We want our students to know that we expect them to use explicit and rich words that are above their spelling level and that it's okay not to have everything spelled perfectly in our nonpublished writing. It is more important to maintain our writing flow and not to lose our thoughts. So underlining and moving on lets us know that we need to revisit the spelling but doesn't stop our good thinking and writing. The lesson sounds something like the following:

"Friends, there is something you need to know that will really help you with your independence, and it's what to do when you want to write a word that you don't know how to spell [Figure 5.4]. Before I show you, let me think about what I want to write about . . . Oh, I know! Last night the weirdest thing happened! I was sitting outside after dinner, reading a book, when a huge owl landed on the railing of my deck. I sat perfectly still, hardly daring to breathe. The owl was staring very intently into the grassy area below. Suddenly, it seemed to fall right off the edge of the deck! I jumped up and ran to the deck's edge just in time to see the owl grab a huge rat and take off flying with it into the air. Woo-hoo! Thank you, owl!

"Okay, there is my plan for what I will write. Now I am ready to get started." Using a chart rack, interactive whiteboard, or paper under a document camera, we begin our story, varying the modeling and language to meet the age of students we are teaching. For instance, we might show young writers how we stretch words out to distinguish the individual sounds in them as we write, or we might show intermediate students how

Figure 5.4
Joan models the strategy of underlining words you don't know how to spell and moving on while writing.

we revise and edit as we go, crossing off a tired word and replacing it with a more specific and interesting word.

After writing "Last night the . . . ," we pause. "Class, I don't know how to spell *weirdest*, but I really want to use that word. Since I have to stay in one place and write the whole time, I'm not going to get up or stop and ask someone; I'm just going to make my best guess, underline it, and go on. I can come back to fix it later." We continue writing, adding "wirdest thing happened." We continue writing in front of the class for just another sentence or so, modeling a couple more times how we make our best guess with tricky words by writing the sounds we hear, underline our attempt, and keep going.

We write about our lives for this Work-on-Writing practice, and rather than get hung up on trying to spell tricky words and stop our writing flow to ask someone how to spell a word, we make our best attempt at spelling them and then underline the words if we think they are spelled wrong. On this first day, that is plenty for students to take in for this lesson.

After a four-minute modeled writing demonstration, we distribute sheets of blank paper. Even though we are not launching Work on Writing at this time, we send students around the room to find places to write. We give those who are not writing at a table a clipboard as well. Students write about anything that happened yesterday or today or over the summer, underlining words they are unsure of. There will be time later in the week to introduce writing notebooks, how to keep track of drafts, and so on. We keep this first piece of writing as an initial writing assessment and sample. Again, once this lesson and practice time is over we give our students a brain and body break. We want to remember the power of brain breaks. Not only are we all tired the first day but also ample brain breaks allow students to be much more successful when we ask them to focus on classroom procedures and learning.

After the brain and body break, it's time to consider another practice round of Read to Self from Daily 5. In these early days, there may be time to practice at three to five different times throughout the day, building the students' stamina as well as their muscle memory for the desired behaviors. We watch again for the barometer child and stop the group as soon as we notice restless behavior, even if it's after only a couple of minutes.

At this point on the first day, we have certainly accomplished a lot! We have already taught the following:

- 3 Ways to Read a Book
- How to Choose Good-Fit Books and I PICK
- Underline Words I Don't Know How to Spell

Moving ahead after the practice of Read to Self, we look again at the list of foundation lessons for the Daily 5. Since we have already chosen lessons from Read to Self and Work on Writing, we choose a foundation lesson for Read to Someone (see also Appendix D).

Read-to-Someone Foundation Lessons
- Check for Understanding
- EEKK (elbow, elbow, knee, knee)
- Voice Level
- How Partners Read
- How to Get Started
- Coaching or Time?
- How to Choose a Partner

Typically our very first Read-to-Someone foundation lesson is one that coincides with the CAFE Menu strategy we have been focusing on: Check for Understanding. Students first heard about and saw this strategy modeled the very first thing in the morning when we taught Three Ways to Read a Book. When we present the strategy of Check for Understanding again in the Read-to-Someone foundation lesson, we read aloud another picture book. During this picture book, we point out the CAFE Menu board (Boushey and Moser 2009), write the Check for Understanding strategy on a card, and post the strategy card. We even have some of the students try their hand at the strategy within the group. With this foundation lesson, we model stopping frequently to Check for Understanding. During this lesson students chime in in front of the whole group, model for the whole class, or practice with a partner the strategy of Check for Understanding.

As the last step in the introduction of Check for Understanding, we tell children that they will use this strategy each time they do Read to Someone this year. This will involve taking turns reading aloud. After one partner reads, the other partner will restate the who and what of what they just heard, thereby checking for understanding. We want students to practice checking for understanding during this foundation lesson, so we put them into partnerships right there in the gathering place, and then we continue to read aloud. We stop the reading periodically. The first time we stop we have one student in each partnership check for understanding while their partner listens in and provides support if necessary. They switch roles the next time we stop reading to check for understanding, so the other partner has their turn.

If there is still time left in the literacy block we will then do another brain and body break before moving into a short lesson using one of the Listen-to-Reading or Word-Work foundation lessons. (Chapter 6 describes each of these lessons in more detail.)

Listen-to-Reading Foundation Lessons
- Set Up the Technology
- Listen and Follow Along
- Manage Fair and Equitable Use with a Limited Number of Devices

Word-Work Foundation Lessons
- Set Up and Clean Up Materials
- Choose Materials to Use
- Choose a Successful Spot

Both Listen to Reading and Word Work involve how to use materials. Regardless of the age of children we teach, we never set up materials or put them away for students. We start teaching the expectations of how we set up and clean up right away on the first day of the year, so our children quickly become independent with all the materials they use throughout the day.

Our standards for Word-Work materials: They need to be free or cheap! The materials we begin the year with are the same ones we end the year with; we try not to introduce new materials during the year. We want the use of materials as tools to be all about the kinesthetic action of manipulating words to secure them in students' long-term memory. If we continue to add new materials to Word Work we must go through the exploration process, taking away from valuable learning time and creating an environment where it is more about the materials than the reason we use them.

When teaching the first foundation lesson for Word Work, we pull out each of the five Word-Work materials—whiteboards, magnet letters, beans/shells, clay in lids, and stamps—from where they are stored in the supply area.

We briefly explain where the materials are housed, places where students can use the materials, and how they should quickly and quietly put them away. We then pick five students at a time and have each group of children go over to the Word-Work storage area. These five students model for the class how to retrieve materials for Word Work and how to take them to a variety of work spaces, such as a place on the floor, near the Word Wall, at a table, and so on. Once they've chosen a work space, they merely take the materials out, pack them back up, and return them. This first practice session is not even about what words students will work with. Instead, the focus is about setting up, cleaning up quickly and correctly, and putting materials away.

We always think through the procedures for using materials prior to the first day of school. This allows us to take the time during the foundation lesson to clearly teach expectations we want to see all year long (cleaning up correctly and in a timely manner, using materials in correct locations, and so on). These behaviors will imprint on students. If we teach something to students in the first few days of the school year, we always try to be certain it will have the outcome we want the rest of the year. Trying to reteach something midyear is very challenging because of the phenomenon we call "beginning-of-the-year imprinting." Just as ducklings will become attached to the first creature they see when they come out of the shell, so students will become attached to classroom procedures they learn at the beginning of the school year! We also know that seeing and doing a task repeatedly is essential in building muscle memory for students.

This chapter has included the foundation lessons we teach on the first day of school as we launch Read to Self. Chapter 6 will take you through the other foundation lessons taught prior to the introduction of the next Daily 5.

Foundation Lessons

The secret of change is to focus all of your energy, not on fighting the old, but on building the new.

—Socrates

Day two of Read to Self closely resembles day one. We continue to work on building stamina and training children's muscle memories. We begin literacy time with a review of yesterday's Read-to-Self lesson, Three Ways to Read a Book. Once the review of Three Ways to Read a Book is completed, it is time to focus on Read to Self. We spend time each day reviewing the I-chart, because these charts will guide our learning throughout the year. We read over each item the class generated and refined the day before, pausing long enough for children to form pictures in their minds.

When students complete the stamina building round of Read to Self our literacy block is not yet over, so we select foundation lessons from each of the Daily 5 to teach. The foundation lessons for each Daily 5 will be taught before that Daily 5 is launched, which is why the launching of Read to Self is so important and different from the launching of the other Daily 5. We are teaching the behaviors of Read to Self along with all the other Daily 5 foundation lessons in the midst of launching Read to Self. In essence, we are building the airplane as we are flying it.

This chapter is devoted to these foundation lessons and is organized by each Daily 5. Appendixes B through F provide a one-page guide to each Daily 5 to support you in launching each Daily 5 component. This chapter is a reference section for you and supplements information you will find elsewhere in this book, including the appendixes. The foundation lessons are not taught all on one day nor will they always be taught in the order they are presented here. Think about the students you have, their immediate needs, and the Daily 5 component you want to introduce next. These factors will dictate the order of lessons you teach and review.

Read-to-Self Foundation Lessons (See Appendix B)

- Three Ways to Read a Book (see Chapter 5, page 68)
- I PICK Good-Fit Books (see Chapter 5, page 73)
- Choose a Successful Spot

Choose a Successful Spot

Before students choose their own place to sit for a Daily 5 round, we teach a focus lesson on how to choose a spot where they can be successful. By the time we begin the discussion, we have helped students try out various places in the room during Read to Self over the course of a few days.

"Each day as we have been practicing and building our stamina, I have been picking your spots for you and placing you around the room. You have experienced many different places and you know where you have stamina and can be successful. Today you will select a spot to read using what you know about best places for you to work. What will you take into consideration before you choose a spot to sit and begin?"

Since students have practiced daily and felt how different spaces feel, they will come up with things like this:

- Sit on chairs or on the floor, as long as we can sit EEKK (see page 92).
- Sit at least an arm's length away from other classmates.
- Leave room for the teacher to confer with us.
- If possible, turn our bodies so our voices will go away from students around us.
- Pick a place that is comfortable so we can build stamina.

Once we have crafted the chart together, we release students to find a spot in the room. Staggering the release of students avoids a stampede and ensures a smooth and orderly start to the practice session. Once the round is complete (as determined by their stamina), we ring the chimes, reflect, and see if there are things we need to add to the chart to make Read to Self even better.

Work-on-Writing Foundation Lessons (See Appendix C)

- Underline Words You Don't Know How to Spell, and Move On (see Chapter 5, page 81)
- Set Up a Notebook
- Choose What to Write About

Set Up a Notebook

We have tried using and teaching children to use every kind of notebook you can imagine: spirals, small spirals, three-ring binders, bound books, expensive books, cheap notebooks, lined books, blank books. We think Ralph Fletcher summed this up best: "When it comes right down to it, a writer's notebook is nothing more than a blank book, but within those pages you've got a powerful tool for writing and living" (1996, 7).

We have settled on notebooks that we can manage and that we can teach children how to manage. For us, loose paper is difficult to keep organized, but we can manage our writing in a spiral or composition notebook. We start the year with class sets of these notebooks, or, if possible, we add them to the student supply list. We explain to the class that we will be writing each day in school during Daily 5 and that they will be keeping their writing together in their writer's notebook, where they can use words, phrases, questions, pictures, or lists to capture their thinking and to express their ideas. Since notebooks are highly individual, students write their name on their cover and find pictures to draw, cut out of magazines, or bring from home depicting things they would like to write about. We also cut the top corners of the first three to five pages of each writer's notebook. This clearly marks the children's list of "think-abouts," described in the next section.

Choose What to Write About

We write to make sense of our lives.

—Steve Boolos

Generating ideas can be the hardest part of the writing process. When it comes to teaching, modeling, and reinforcing the task of finding ideas and choosing a topic, we talk to students about what Neil Gaiman (1997) does: "I make the ideas up. Out of my head." We can take the complex task of facing a blank sheet of paper and partner it with the strategy of the "think-about." The lesson we call Think-About helps students get past the blank sheet and come up with a writing topic.

The lessons sounds like this: "Class, when trying to come up with ideas of what to write about, we first notice the ideas in our head and then do what's called a think-about.

"This strategy is important because it gets your brain thinking about ideas in your head. Once you have an idea, you think about it, and that becomes what you write about. For example, right now I notice that one idea in my head is my dog, Tana. The first pages of our notebook are where we will be keeping our ideas of what to write about. I'm going to start by making a title for this place in my writer's notebook." At the top of the page we write "What to Write About," and then we continue with the lesson. "Since I'm thinking about my dog, I'm going to write 'Tana' here, but that's not all I'm going to write. I'm going to *think about* this topic and jot down all the things I do with Tana." If we are using a document camera, we model this on the first page of our notebook:

Tana:
Walking the trails
Giving her a bath
Teaching her tricks

"Now I take a moment and notice that Tana is not the only idea in my head. Lunch is in my head as well. Again, I'm going to use the think-about strategy and I'm going to write in my notebook:"

Lunch:
My new lunchbox
What I'm eating for lunch
What's for hot lunch tomorrow
My favorite thing to put in my lunch

"Right now, I want you to take a quiet moment and notice what is in your head." At this juncture we have two choices; what we choose to do depends on the class or some of the students in our group. If they are a very auditory group, it will be helpful to have them turn and talk, each partner describing what is in his or her head. If you think your students don't need to turn and talk first, you can go right to this next step:

"Turn to the first page of your notebook and, just like I did, write down what is in your head." We use this strategy with very young and ELL students as well; the difference is that we model using pictures instead of or along with writing words.

"Now, think about what's in your head, just like I did with Tana and lunch. What other ideas do you have about that topic in your head? Write down your ideas, just like I did.

"Turn to your elbow buddy and read your idea as well as what you wrote for the think-about." We have students share with partners, as this will often give others more ideas of what to write about.

We continue with this process for a few more minutes. Then we wrap up this lesson by saying, "We will continue to add to our 'What to Write About' pages all year long. There will be times that something happens at home and you come into class talking about it. We will all help each other remember to make it a habit to write down what happened in our notebooks on the 'What to Write About' pages, and to record our think-abouts as well. That way if you are ever facing a blank page during Work on Writing during Daily 5 and you aren't sure what to write about, you can turn to these pages and see all the ideas you have written down and you will always have something to write about!"

Read-to-Someone Foundation Lessons
(See Appendix D)

■ ■ ■ ■ ■ ■   EEKK (elbow, elbow, knee, knee)
  ■   Voice Level
  ■   Check for Understanding
  ■   How Partners Read
  ■   How to Get Started
  ■   Coaching or Time?
  ■   How to Choose a Partner

EEKK (Elbow, Elbow, Knee, Knee)

EEKK is an acronym for elbow, elbow, knee, knee. It represents the way we want our students to sit with each other when they do partner work. Having children sit this way allows for easier book sharing, a quiet voice level, and helpful partner coaching, since both partners can see and follow along with the text.

In our primary classrooms, the lesson sounds something like this: "Before we brainstorm the behaviors of Read to Someone, we need to learn a couple of tricks for being good reading partners. As you know, my sister doesn't like spiders. What do you suppose she says and does when she sees a spider?"

"I scream, so I bet she screams!" replies Jolie.

"She sure does. She says 'EEKK!' And then do you know what she does? She moves over, really close to me. She sits right by my side, elbow to elbow, knee to knee. Jolie, would you come sit right up here beside me and pretend you are my sister who has just seen a spider?" Jolie and I sit on the floor, or in chairs, right next to each other so that one of her elbows is next to one of my elbows and one of her knees is next to one of my knees, almost touching. Then, Jolie and I place a book between us, so she is holding one side and I am holding the other. The rest of this lesson is described in the next section, "Voice Level."

In our intermediate or middle school classrooms, we share the EEKK acronym and discuss the purposes for sitting side by side with our knees and elbows together, then model, leaving out the spider story.

Voice Level

After modeling how to hold the book, we talk about voice level. "See how easy it is for the two of us to share a book when we sit this way? Listen how quiet our voices can be when we sit this close." I begin to read to Jolie in a very soft voice. "Jolie, can you hear me even though I am reading to you in a very soft voice?" The lack of volume influences her response and the typically gregarious and expressive Jolie merely nods. "Garrett, you are sitting the farthest from us. Can you hear my voice as I read to Jolie?"

He replies, "No."

"When we use a voice that is just for our partner, we are using a private voice. We use a private voice when we want our partner to hear us, but don't want to distract those around us from the hard work they are doing."

Michael Grinder (1995) has helped us understand that the loudest voice in the room is the one that regulates the noise level. Therefore, we intentionally model a very soft voice when we show children how to read to someone. When we model most-desirable and least-desirable behaviors, we reinforce this expectation as well.

We continue to monitor our own voice level all year long. We are careful to keep our voices quiet when we confer with children and work with a small group. We rarely want our voices to be the loudest in the room.

Check for Understanding

We introduce this strategy on the first day of school and review it many times in the following few weeks. "Whenever I read to myself, I stop to check for understanding. It's a strategy that really helps me understand what I read. Check for Understanding is something we'll do with a partner as well. Emily and I are going to show you what it looks like and sounds like.

"Emily, you get to start reading out loud first. You are going to read with your eyes, brain, and voice, but I am just going to use my eyes and brain. When you finish the first page, stop, and I'll check for understanding."

When Emily finishes the page, she stops and looks up. If we are teaching primary students, we hold up a visual reminder to check for understanding. One of Joan's parents made wooden check marks for her students (see Figure 6.1). Gail's students use a plastic version called a Check-A-Roo from Learning Loft, Inc.

"To check for understanding means to summarize by restating the 'who' and 'what' of what you just read or heard. Who is it about and what is happening?" We model by saying, "Emily, I just heard you read that there were three bears who lived in a forest and they were going to eat their porridge for breakfast, but it was too hot. So they decided to go for a walk to let it cool down."

Figure 6.1
Partners may use a check mark to remind them to check for understanding.

Photo courtesy of Jon & Moch Photography.

Emily indicates that this is correct. "Now, boys and girls, Emily and I are going to switch jobs. I am going to read with my eyes, brain, and voice, and Emily is going to read with her eyes and brain and be ready to check for understanding." I hand Emily the check mark, and after I read the next page, she checks for the "who" and "what" in the story. We switch roles again, but this time, I do not correctly summarize the gist of the reading. Emily responds, "That's not what I read."

We explain to the class, "Emily told me that I did not understand and remember what she just read. When that happens, she rereads the page to help me understand better. This time I listen very carefully, trying to remember what she just read so I can check for understanding." Emily rereads the page, and this time I summarize it correctly.

After we finish the demonstration, we ask students to tell an elbow buddy what the listener's job is when the reader is reading.

Older students will check for understanding as well, but may or may not need the concrete reminder of a physical check mark to hold. Since many of our older students are using chapter books when they do Read to

Someone, we often first model Check for Understanding after each paragraph and then build our skills gradually to checking after an entire page.

How Partners Read

Partners have a variety of choices when doing Read to Someone together:

Same Book:

- *I Read, You Read.* One student reads a paragraph or a page, then the partner reads the next paragraph or page. A variation on this strategy is to have one person read a paragraph and the partner read the same paragraph. This second strategy is especially useful when working on fluency. The more fluent readers read first. This enables the less fluent readers to hear the pace, intonation, and correct words as a model before they read.

- *Choral Read.* Partners read the same section of the book at the same time. This is a useful strategy to support challenged readers if they are partnered with someone who is just a step ahead of them in their reading.

Different Books:

- I Read, You Read. Each student holds and reads from a good-fit book of their own. One partner places a bookmark or thumb in his or her own book, holding the spot. This partner attends to the second partner's book, listening, reading along, and checking for understanding. The partners reverse roles after each turn. This may seem confusing, but students typically manage this very well, and because a culture of kindness, support, and respect has been well established, it does not matter if the levels of the books vary in difficulty (Figure 6.2).

Figure 6.2
Two students do
Read to
Someone.

Photo courtesy of Gelfand-P per Photography.

How to Get Started

Students sometimes have difficulty agreeing on a shared text or who gets to begin. We teach them a few strategies for making this decision quickly so they can get started right away:

- *Good Manners.* One partner simply says, "Would you like to start first?" The other partner says, "Yes, thank you."
- *Let's Make a Deal.* When two partners both want to read a favorite book, one partner quickly says, "How about if we read your book together first and then we can read mine together."
- *Rock, Paper, Scissors.* The winner gets to choose which book partners read first, or who reads from their book first. It may be important to articulate that it is best out of one, not best out of three or five, so that students don't get distracted playing repeated rounds of the game.
- *Youngest First.* Determine by birthday which partner is the youngest. The youngest gets to choose and begin first.
- *Alphabetical Order.* Partners look at the first letter of their first names. The one that comes first in the alphabet gets to choose and begin first.

Coaching or Time?

When partner reading, students may quickly provide a word when their partner pauses. We nip this overeager helpfulness in the bud with a lesson on how to be a beneficial reading coach.

"How many of you play a sport like soccer, baseball, basketball, or any others?" Many students raise their hands. "What person helps you know what to do while you are playing?"

The class chimes in with, "The coach!"

"Yes, a coach is a person who can give you help when you need it, tells you 'you can do it,' and gives you support. Today we are going to learn a bit about being a reading coach. Put your thumb up if you have ever been reading with a partner and have come to a word you didn't know."

Sierra, a reluctant reader in our classroom, says, "Sometimes the partner just says the word for me, even though I was trying to figure it out on my own."

"Have any of the rest of you had that same thing happen?" Heads nod enthusiastically. "How many of you wish that your partner would give you a chance to try to figure it out on your own using your strategies?" Again, children nod in agreement.

"But sometimes when I am really stuck on a word, I like it when my partner helps me," offers Matthew.

"Good point, Matthew. The trick is to know when someone wants help and when that person wants to do it alone. Think about when you are playing a sport such as baseball. There are times when the coach will come up behind you and really help you, showing you how to hold the bat and swing at the ball. Other times, the coach may just encourage you, not stepping in to help you at all. It is very similar in reading. Sometimes when you get stuck on a word, you want to try to figure it out on your own. Other times you'd like a clue or hint to help you figure it out. Helpful reading coaches don't blurt the word out right away, because that won't help their partner be a better reader.

"Here is what it looks like and sounds like to be a helpful reading coach." We begin a new chart with the title "Reading Coach" on the top.

"When your partner comes to a word he or she doesn't know, you are going to count to three, silently, to yourself." On the chart we write "Silently count to three." We model the speed of the counting by visually showing the count with our fingers.

"After you silently count to three, ask your partner, 'Do you want coaching or time?'" We add this question to the chart.

"If your partner says, 'Time,' you must sit patiently and wait. But while you wait, you have an important job to do. Look carefully at the word. See if you can figure out what strategy would best help your partner figure it out. That way, you'll be ready if they change their mind.

"If your partner says, 'Coaching,' you will suggest a strategy that you think will help them the most."

There are several ways to provide students with a coaching tip sheet. A bookmark, sheet in a notebook, anchor chart, or the CAFE Menu are all ways to provide coaches with strategy reminders. Whichever we provide, we add it to the Reading Coach chart. If we provide students with a bookmark that lists coaching tips, for example, we write "Refer to Coaching Bookmark" on the chart.

"Let's practice. Kennedy, would you like to model?" We take the coaching bookmark and ask Kennedy to get a book from her book box, read a bit, and then find a word that she either doesn't know or can pretend not to know. When she comes to the word she doesn't know, we go through the coaching steps, thinking aloud to show the rest of the class what we would do with Kennedy.

"Oh, Kennedy is stuck on a word. I'll count silently to three to give her some time to figure it out." We count silently, putting a finger up with each mental number. After the count of a very slow three (about one count every two seconds), we ask softly, "Kennedy, would you like time or coaching?"

Kennedy says, "Time." We continue to let the class know what we are thinking.

"Kennedy wants time to figure this word out, but I am going to look at the word and my coaching strategies to see what might work best if she changes her mind. Let's see . . ." We look at the word and look over the strategies, nodding when we have an idea, then wait patiently.

We are ready when Kennedy says, "I changed my mind. May I have coaching, please?"

"Yes, it is a big word, but it is really two words put together. Break it in half and see if you can get it."

Kennedy puts her finger over the second half, reads the first chunk, then reads the second chunk, then gleefully puts them together.

"Class, did you notice that our coaching helped Kennedy figure this word out on her own? That is the goal of coaching!"

We ask Kennedy to continue reading, but this time to ask for coaching right away so we can show what that would look like. When she stops, we model, without thinking aloud this time. We count to three silently but with our fingers and then ask, "Do you want coaching or time?"

She says, "Coaching."

We refer to our coaching sheet and say, "Kennedy, have you tried 'Back Up and Reread'?" She says she has but that it didn't work. "Okay, how about skipping the word and coming back to it?" When she skips it, the following words clue her in. Kennedy backs up, rereads correctly, and continues.

"Coaching our friends with a helpful strategy instead of giving them the word is the best way to help them grow as readers," we reiterate.

Each of the reading strategies is taught individually and added to the coaching bookmark as they are added to the CAFE Menu. As the year progresses and the strategies become intuitive, the need to refer to the coaching sheet becomes unnecessary and students will refer to the CAFE Menu that is posted in the room.

How to Choose a Partner

During the first few days of the launching phase for Read to Someone, we have matched students with their partners. But because we want students to be independent, after just a few days of practicing Read to Someone we begin teaching them how to quietly, kindly, and expediently select partners on their own.

The lesson sounds something like this: "Class, I have been matching you with a partner as we've been building our stamina and practicing the behaviors of Read to Someone. Today we will learn one way to find your own partner. The great thing about it is that it works anytime you need a partner. So, whether you need a partner for Read to Someone, a math game, a science experiment, or anything else, you'll want to know how to do this.

"When we choose partners, it is very important to remember that our partner doesn't always need to be our very closest friend. In fact, sometimes our very closest friends don't make the best partners, because we might have a tendency to visit instead of read. We will discover new books, new reading interests, and new friendships when we meet with different people often.

"When it comes time to choose a partner, we want to communicate to the group that we need one, but what do you think would happen if we just started yelling, 'Hey, I need a partner!'" The class giggles. At this point in the year, they are becoming accustomed to the soft tone of our rooms, so the intrusion of a loud voice yelling for a partner is out of place and even a bit uncomfortable. "Well, that obviously isn't a good idea! So, here are the steps we'll follow to find a partner." We introduce a new anchor chart, entitled "How to Choose a Partner," which we have prepared ahead of time. As we point out and read each item on the chart, we explain a bit about it.

1. Mouth stays closed. Hand goes up. "This is a silent signal that shows we are in need of a partner."
2. Calmly walk to a nearby classmate whose hand is raised. "We don't need to fly across the room when someone in need of a partner is close by."
3. Make eye contact. "Looking a friend right in the eye shows they have our attention." (See Figure 6.3.)
4. Ask politely. "Saying in a voice that is positive and friendly, 'Will you be my partner?' is inviting and feels good."
5. Partner smiles and responds, "Yes, thank you." "When the partner smiles and replies, 'Yes, thank you,' it is positive and feels good."

"The tone of voice is very important in our classroom. Madeline, will you help me model this? I am going to ask you to be my partner in a few different ways, and I want you to tell me how they feel." First we ask with

Photo courtesy of Jon & Moch Photography.

Figure 6.3
Fifth graders
practice
choosing a
partner.

a monotone voice and no smile. Madeline remarks that it doesn't feel bad, but it doesn't feel good either. Then we ask with a frown and a grumpy tone of voice, as if she were the only one left and not the person we had in mind when we selected Read to Someone. This one definitely does not feel good. Her response is, "I don't feel like you really want to be my partner at all." Finally, we smile, and sincerely ask, "Madeline, would you please be my partner?" This one accomplishes the goal, because she says, "Now I feel like you want to read with me, and I really want to read with you, too. I'm sorry this is just pretend!"

"Boys and girls," we continue, "that is how we always want our partners to feel—like we are really excited to read with them, because then they will be excited about reading with us, too!"

Then we have students practice in groups of about six at a time, until everyone in the class has had a chance to practice. We are very purposeful about giving every child in the class a chance to model putting his or her hand up, making eye contact, walking to a partner, asking to be partners, and responding with a nice tone of voice. This can be challenging for our shy students, and we watch them closely for a few days to see if they need support. After they have a few positive interactions, they are ready to do it on their own.

Listen-to-Reading Foundation Lessons (See Appendix E)

■ ■ ■ ■ ■ ■ Set Up and Clean Up the Technology
        ■ Listen and Follow Along
        ■ Manage Fairness and Equitable Use with a Limited Number of Devices

Set Up and Clean Up the Technology

Listening devices such as computers, notebooks, CD players, and tape recorders all require certain set-up procedures. And they need to be returned to their original state so they are ready for the next user. Many teachers have access to stories on the Internet, so loading these web addresses or applications will make for a smooth start to Listen to Reading. Be sure you take the time to explicitly teach and model the set-up and cleanup procedures for every device you have available for Listen to Reading. Have children practice with your supervision before they try it on their own.

Figure 6.4
A student listens to an audiobook on an iPad.

Photo courtesy of Gelfand-Piper Photography.

Listen and Follow Along

We teach children to follow along with their eyes and/or finger as they listen to a story. We cue students into the words that are being read in all stories, whether they're listening to a tape while holding a book or following the highlighted words on a computer screen.

Manage Fairness and Equitable Use

We use computers and e-readers with audio capability for Listen to Reading (Figure 6.4). Because we have a limited number of devices, we divide the class by the number of devices and create lists of students who will share each device. We teach children that when their story is finished they should return to the home screen and pass the device on to the next person on the list. Once they are finished with their turn at Listen to Reading and hand off their device, they move into Read to Self.

Word-Work Foundation Lessons (See Appendix F)

■ ■ ■ ■ ■ ■ Set Up and Clean Up Materials
■ Choose Materials and Words to Use
■ Choose a Successful Spot

Set Up and Clean Up Materials

Take time to introduce each of the materials that are available for the student to use for Word Work and where each is stored in the room. Model and have students practice how to gather and correctly use each of the materials and how to return the materials to the correct spot.

Choose Materials and Words to Use

It is important to teach students that not all materials will be used by all students. Encourage students to think about the materials as they use them in order to determine which materials actually help them to remember the words they are practicing. Some may find writing the words on the whiteboard over and over while saying the letters and, finally, reading the word helps them know the word, whereas using magnetic letters is fun but doesn't achieve the desired skill of being able to remember the words.

You will need to decide on and inform students about which words they each will practice and where to find the words they will be practicing. For students who need to work with words, model setting up materials near the word wall or near the class word collector to practice common sight words or class vocabulary words (Figure 6.5). For other students, model how they might use words they are misspelling in their writing.

Choose a Successful Spot

As with Read to Self, students will need to be taught how to choose a spot where they and others can be successful. Once students have been taught this skill during the Read-to-Self launch, you may just need to review the I-chart and direct the students' attention to the skills they already have for

Figure 6.5
This word collector is an organized way to visually display the words that we learn through our read-alouds, content areas, and community conversations.

Photo courtesy of Jon & Moch Photography.

choosing a spot for Read to Self. Then, add behaviors as needed to the chart for Word Work. We find that the behaviors truly are the same.

In this new edition of *The Daily 5*, we spend a considerable amount of time focusing on foundation lessons. These foundation lessons allow for the preteaching of behaviors that will pave the way for a smooth and concise launching of each of the Daily 5 choices found in the next chapter.

When to Launch the Next Daily 5

Don't save something for a special occasion. Every day of your life is a special occasion.

—Thomas S. Monson

Read to Self is launched, and students are building stamina every day. Skills for the remaining Daily 5 choices are being successfully added to students' repertoire with each foundation lesson. How do we know when to launch the next Daily 5 choice?

We introduce students to the next Daily 5 choice when they demonstrate independence and increased stamina during Read to Self. We watch for them to demonstrate the I-chart behaviors consistently and to maintain stamina for a length of time that correlates approximately with their ages.

- Intermediate students: 12–14 minutes of stamina
- Primary students: 10–12 minutes of stamina
- Kindergarten students: 7–8 minutes of stamina

When using minutes of stamina as our marker for when to introduce the next Daily 5, we can keep track of the increasing class stamina by graphing the minutes the class engages in reading independently during each practice time. When we graph the number of minutes of stamina our students have each day, it makes the stamina time visual and thus more tangible (Figure 3.7).

Even with the preceding criteria (consistent demonstration of I-chart behaviors and appropriate amount of stamina), it is important to remember that Daily 5 is very flexible. There isn't just one right way, nor should you feel you have to strictly adhere to the stamina minute guidelines we give.

When adding the next Daily 5 choice, keep in mind that every year each class is different. There have been years when it only takes four days for the class to show us they are ready to launch the next Daily 5. But we have also had years in which it took thirteen days until we felt they were ready. Therefore, when getting Daily 5 up and running, we always use this statement as our Daily 5 mantra: "Don't worry about what last year's group did or what my teaching partners' classes are doing. It is all about this group of students. What are they capable of and what do they need most right now? And remember, they are giving us everything they have."

Once students meet the required number of minutes of stamina for Read to Self, we prepare to launch Work on Writing the following day. As mentioned in Chapter 1, we launch Work on Writing as the second Daily 5 choice rather than Read to Someone (as stated in the first edition of *The Daily 5*). Work on Writing is so important, we want to get it up and running as soon as possible.

Launching Work on Writing

■ ■ ■ ■ ■ The writing component of the Daily 5 provides additional time for students to practice and become proficient writers. Its purpose is to provide daily writing time, with choice playing an important role.

Writing workshop and Work on Writing within Daily 5 are not the same. During writing workshop we may teach a specific type of writing students must learn based on our current unit of study. Children often use Work on Writing time within Daily 5 to continue work they are doing during writing workshop, but not always. They thoroughly enjoy the freedom of choice that is part of Daily 5. It is then that they may do sustained writing of any form they like. Here are some examples:

- Persuasive writing, convincing friends to read a favorite book or see a popular movie
- Friendly letters to a classmate, pen pal, or relative
- Recounts and narratives of personal stories, such as a lost tooth, a family vacation, or the loss of a beloved pet
- Reports on topics of current interest
- Music and poetry
- Procedural writing

On the day we launch Work on Writing, we start by reviewing our Read to Self I-chart and building stamina in Read to Self. Once this is done, we excitedly tell our class that today is the day we will be adding another choice to Daily 5, Work on Writing.

We begin, as always, by setting the purpose for this element of the Daily 5. "Today we are going to begin our very first day of Work on Writing. We will be doing Work on Writing every day. [See step 1 of the 10 Steps to Independence, page 36.] Turn to an elbow buddy and talk over why you think it is so important to work on writing." By the time we introduce Work on Writing to the class, many students will see the connection between the Read to Self expectations and those of Work on Writing. The resulting conversation sounds something like this:

"Who would like to share what their partner said about why it is important to write every day?"

Scott: "Madeline said because it is the best way to become a better writer." As Scott says this, he glances at the I-chart for Read to Self that is hanging in our gathering place. He has made the connection between the sense of urgency for Read to Self and Work on Writing.

Jolie: "Mark said we write every day because it is fun!"

To establish a purpose and sense of urgency, we add the reasons to a new I-chart for Work on Writing (Figure 7.1). (See step 2 of the 10 Steps to Independence, page 36.)

Next, we brainstorm with students the behaviors for writing independently.

Because a similar launching activity has been done with Read to Self, students have a good idea of what working independently on writing will look and sound like. Often the class will quickly articulate the behaviors independent writers will exhibit, and we write them on the I-chart. If students do not volunteer some of the ideas we want (see the sample I-chart in Figure 7.1), we elicit the ideas by reviewing the Read-to-Self chart or simply list the desired behaviors ourselves. It is exciting to hear children chime right in when filling out the teacher side of the I-chart. They understand that we will be actively engaged with children, teaching them individually or in small groups. (See step 3 of the 10 Steps to Independence.)

"Now, who can show us how to do Work on Writing the correct way?" We watch while one or two students get their book boxes (which contain their writer's notebooks), find a nearby spot, and model writing independently in front of the whole class. As they model, we check for independence by referring to each item on the I-chart, finishing with the

Figure 7.1
The I-chart for Work on Writing is very similar to the I-chart for Read to Self.

Photo courtesy of Jon & Moch Photography.

question, "Class, if _____ continues to do these things, will he or she become a better writer?" (See step 4 of the 10 Steps to Independence.)

After the demonstration of desired behaviors, we invite a volunteer to model undesired behaviors. We select someone we suspect will have difficulty staying engaged during Work on Writing. As they clown around, sharpen a pencil, and waste precious writing time during their demonstration, we refer to the I-chart, then end with, "Class, if _____ continues to do these things, will he or she become a better writer?" Since the answer is no, and we want everyone to remember what it truly looks like when a student is being successful, the same student moves right into the correct model. They are retraining their muscle memory, showing what they will need to do to become a better writer, raising the level of accountability for everyone. (See step 5 of the 10 Steps to Independence.)

Now it's time for everyone to practice. For the first few days of launching Work on Writing, we place children around the room just as we did when we launched Read to Self. We call students in groups of four or five, and after they've retrieved their book boxes (which contain their writer's notebooks and a pen or pencil), we show them all the different places a writer may sit. By this time in the school year, we know exactly who has the greatest stamina and independence, so wc begin placing our most independent children first, saving those with the shortest stamina for last— their practice time is often slightly shorter. (See step 6 of the 10 Steps to Independence.)

Students begin writing immediately after being seated, and we stay out of the way, all the while keeping track of the time and watching for a break in stamina. As soon as someone goes off task and fails to get back on immediately, we give the signal to regroup at the gathering place for a review of the I-chart and some self-reflection. (See steps 7 and 8 of the 10 Steps to Independence.)

As we refer to the I-chart, students rate themselves by holding one, two, three, or four fingers up for each criteria. Stamina is marked on a stamina chart, and a new goal for time and improved behaviors is set prior to another practice. This goal-setting is typically done together as a whole class. Often the class will have such enthusiasm that they will want the goal to be an unreasonable amount, and students will call out, "We can write for twenty minutes!" We gently remind them about the story of building stamina when running—in other words, we set small goals to be sure we can be successful. (See steps 9 and 10 of the 10 Steps to Independence.) At this time, older students may have enough stamina to review the I-chart and practice again. For younger students, that may be all for now. When we launch Read to Self, it isn't unusual for students to have a small amount of stamina. By the time we launch Work on Writing, students have more stamina and can engage with their writing for a longer period of time.

Introducing Choice

■ ■ ■ ■ ■ Each day we continue to practice Read to Self and Work on Writing until Work on Writing stamina has increased to the number of minutes (see list at the start of this chapter) that indicate that students are securing the desired behaviors. It is then time to introduce choice (Figure 7.2). It can be tempting to postpone this, especially when things are going so well with our whole class practicing Read to Self at the same time and then moving on to Work on Writing. It seems so tidy and organized, and we are reluctant to mess with a good thing. However, we believe that children become more engaged, motivated, and successful when they have choice, not only over what they read and write but also over the order in which they participate in those activities. So, even though it can be difficult at first to give up being in control of their literacy choices, the payoff is always immense. It always makes us laugh when we think we are actually giving up control. After all, we have taught them to be independent; what are we really giving up?

Figure 7.2
These students have chosen the order in which they'll do Read to Self and Work on Writing.

Photo courtesy of Gelfand-Piper Photography.

If we stop to think about it, we are more motivated, engaged, and productive when we are in control of our schedules. We know the expectations of our jobs and want to be trusted to choose the order of our daily tasks and the approaches we take to completing them. Why should our children feel any differently? This, we believe, is at the heart of choice: knowing the expectations, possessing the skills to meet them, being trusted to carry them out, and taking the responsibility to do so. It is what we desire and provide for our students.

The day we introduce choice is always an exciting one, and the lesson sounds something like this:

"Class, we are so excited about our day today. You have learned how to be independent when you do Read to Self and Work on Writing. Today you will be completely in charge of the order in which you do those. Some of you may choose Read to Self first, others may choose Work on Writing. You all know why you are doing each choice and how to work independently. We trust you to be independent during the time you work on your Daily 5 choice just as you have learned and practiced."

Dan, with his eyes sparkling, says, "You mean you aren't going to tell us what to do?"

"No," we respond. "We trust you to make a choice that feels right to your brain and body. Dan, what do you feel like starting with today?"

"Yesterday I was writing a story about scoring a goal in my soccer game; I wanted to finish it then but didn't have time. Could I finish it now?"

"Absolutely," we say. "Class, take a few moments to think about which Daily 5 you would like to begin with. Make a picture in your mind of what your body looks like, sounds like, and feels like while you're engaged in that choice."

At this time, we grab our Daily 5 Check-In form (Figure 7.3). We describe its use in the next section.

Check-In

Once independence and stamina have been established, the purpose of check-in shifts from having students reflect on their behaviors to answering the question, "What are you doing today?" Atwell calls this the "status-of-the-class conference" (1998, 89) and explains that taking three minutes to poll children about what each is doing that round creates immediate focus on the child's work and is time well spent. Every session, each student's response is recorded on a form like the one in Figure 7.3.

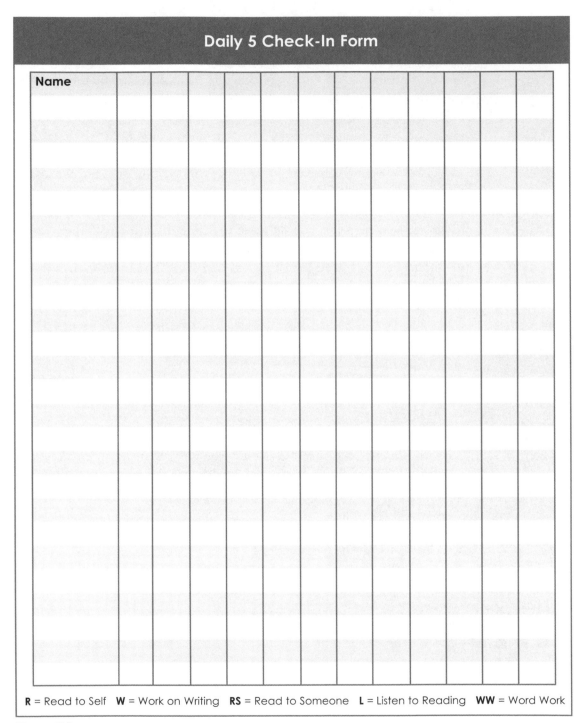

Daily 5 Check-In Form

Name												

R = Read to Self   **W** = Work on Writing   **RS** = Read to Someone   **L** = Listen to Reading   **WW** = Word Work

Figure 7.3
We use this check-in form to keep track of each Daily 5 choice students make over the course of a week.

One by one, we ask students what they've chosen to work on first. When Nathan says, "Work on Writing," we place a W in the first box beside his name. When Michelle says, "Read to Self," we place an R in the first box next to her name. An additional choice is added with each successful launch of another Daily 5 activity, and check-in will eventually include the following choices and their codes:

- Read to Self = R
- Work on Writing = W
- Read to Someone = RS
- Listen to Reading = L
- Word Work = WW

Once all Daily 5 choices are up and running, prior to calling names for student choices, we let students know whom we are going to work with in a small group or individually. This eliminates the frustration and disappointment of making a choice and being called away from it. So, we might say, "This round, I am going to work with Marcel and Stella. Would you two grab your book boxes, join me in the gathering area, and start reading?"

When children verbalize their choices, there is a sense of increased accountability. They take the choice very seriously, get started right away, and stick with it.

After assessments have been completed and we have identified goals and strategies for each student, they articulate this information when they check in with their choice. For example, as we call on students for check-in, it sounds something like this (note that the strategies mentioned here are from *The CAFE Book* (Boushey and Moser 2009):

"Katie?"

"I am going to do Read to Self. My goal is comprehension, and I am going to Check for Understanding."

"Jonathan?"

"I am going to do Read to Self. My goal is accuracy and I am going to use Cross Checking."

"Sammi?"

"I am going to do Work on Writing. My goal is conventions. I am going to make sure I have an end mark at the end of each sentence."

In order to speed up the process of checking in, we always call students in the same order (Jonathan always follows Katie; Sammi always follows Jonathan), starting at a different child in the list each day.

Releasing Students into Daily 5

■ ■ ■ ■ ■ Prior to releasing students after they make their Daily 5 choices, we make sure there is an even number of students for Read to Someone. If we have an odd number, a student may opt out to make it even, or another student might opt in, and occasionally our younger students will happily read to a stuffed animal or puppet for a partner. Once students have checked in, there are a few options for releasing them to the next round.

1. Unless they chose Read to Someone, students are dismissed individually right after they check in, moving directly into their choice and getting started right away. This minimizes their wait time in the group and staggers the release. Read-to-Someone students can be matched as soon as pairs become available, or at the end, once all the other students have been dismissed.
2. Students all remain in the gathering place and are excused in groups. "If you chose Read to Self, you may go and get started." Pause. "If you chose Work on Writing, you may go and get started." Pause . . . and so on. Save the Read-to-Someone students for last, ending with, "If you chose Read to Someone, find a partner and get started."
3. Students remain in the gathering space and are released all at once. When our friend Lori does this, it looks and sounds like this: She holds up one finger and says, "One." The class get quiet, thinking about where they are going to go and what it will look like and sound like when they get started right away. As she stands, she quietly says, "Two," and holds up two fingers. The class stands, and watches her hand. She does not say anything, but when she raises her third finger, students silently and calmly move to a successful spot and get started. Students who need a partner find one quickly. She remains frozen for about twenty seconds, and then she and the students she has chosen to work with settle in for their work time together.

Read to Someone

■ ■ ■ ■ ■ Of all the choices children participate in, Read to Someone is often the favorite (see Figure 7.4). Reading with someone helps readers, especially developing readers, increase in areas of comprehension, accuracy, fluency, and expressiveness. It also increases reading involvement, attention, and collaboration. What's more, children love partner reading and readily par-

Figure 7.4
When behaviors
of Read to
Someone are
explicitly taught,
it can be highly
successful and
engaging.

ticipate with books of their choosing. They enjoy thinking and learning together. Read to Someone increases the following:

- Quantity of reading
- Level of attention to reading
- Reading motivation
- Opportunity to practice skills and strategies
- Fluency
- Expression
- Reading rate
- Word-attack skills
- Vocabulary
- Love of reading

Some teachers, believing in its importance, have tried partner reading only to feel frustrated with the increased noise level. We'll share a few strategies that will enable your students to derive the benefits from partner reading and enable you not only to maintain your sanity but also to enjoy this choice.

We introduce Read to Someone by following the same 10 Steps to Independence that we followed for Read to Self and Work on Writing. Children get very excited about this addition. We know that explicit teaching and practice is required if we are to keep this choice an engaging and productive partnership instead of chaos. We've found that the key to the success of Read to Someone is ensuring students have internalized the series of foundation lessons that provide them with the skills they will need to listen carefully to their peers, offer assistance, and share materials fairly. The explicit teaching and practicing of these skills has made all the difference in the quality of the social interactions our students have as they read with partners as well as work with partners throughout the day. Because of the lengthy list of foundation lessons for Read to Someone, it is often the very last of the Daily 5 choices we introduce.

Listen to Reading

Listen to Reading is extremely popular in primary grades and is also an option for intermediate students. Listen to Reading provides pronunciation and expression models that can only come from hearing fluent and expressive examples. Because of this, Listen to Reading is especially beneficial for our older struggling readers whose listening comprehension far exceeds their actual reading level. It is also a great resource for our high population of English language learners. We use reading devices such as e-books, computers, tablets, and MP3 players. Audiobooks are often available from public libraries, and the Internet offers rich and wonderful opportunities. (We also keep a list of current and updated resources on our subscription-based website, www.thedailycafe.com.) We launch Listen to Reading following the 10 Steps to Independence.

As students practice, we pay close attention to who is technologically proficient. If necessary, these students can be assigned the role of tech support. This ensures that we can continue working with small groups and individuals during a round of Daily 5 without having to stop to help someone login, find "play," or deal with any other technology issue. As time goes on, everyone becomes proficient at using the Listen-to-Reading tools.

We've found that there is very little need to build stamina for Listen to Reading. Listening to reading is so engaging for children that most have no

Figure 7.5
The number of computers in this classroom determines the number of students who can do Listen to Reading at one time.

problem sticking with it for an extended period of time. Here are the most important things to remember about Listen to Reading:

1. Not everyone does Listen to Reading or needs to.
2. Opportunities and options are limited by the kinds of devices we have and the number available. At Walt Disney Elementary School in Rochester, New York, Holly, a fourth-grade teacher, has an iPad for each of her students so they all can do Listen to Reading at the same time. But just down the hall, Maureen, a second-grade teacher, is limited to five computers for her entire class (Figure 7.5).

Word Work

During Word Work we focus on spelling and vocabulary work with children, creating a richly literate environment that provides essential and often-skipped practice time. Students experiment with spelling patterns, memorize high-frequency words, and develop a genuine curiosity and interest in new and unique words. By playing with words, word patterns, word families, prefixes, suffixes, and so on, students hone their knowledge of words and increase their writing skills. They select from a variety of materials (Figure 7.6), such as these:

- Whiteboards. We have small, lap-sized boards for individual students. They are free to use the classroom whiteboard as well.
- Magnetic letters. We prefer a lowercase set, since that is how most words will be spelled in students' own reading and writing.
- Clay. Modeling clay can be rolled and manipulated into letters or smoothed flat into a container lid, where students can write with a golf tee, then erase with their fingers.
- Letter stamps. We haven't met a child yet who doesn't enjoy rubber stamps.
- Shells. These came from Hawaiian necklaces that we didn't wear; we cut the shells off. Students line them up to form letters for words.
- Technology. Electronic notebooks or iPads. There are a variety of free or inexpensive apps that provide opportunities for children to practice spelling.
- Colored markers. Writing words in different colors, sometimes referred to as rainbow writing, is a favorite Word-Work activity.

These materials in no way represent a list of what you must have or what you should buy. Our rule of thumb is they have to be free or cheap. So use what you have on hand or what you can scrounge from somewhere else. As the Daily 5 holds no content, you will not find a list of spelling words or vocabulary words in this book to use for Word Work. The words we use vary. In our primary grades our focus is on high-frequency words and words students use often that have specific meaning to them (the name of their town, family members, favorite sports or activities, etc.). Practicing these words supports children's writing, fluency, and reading. With older students, the words often come from their personal spelling words, personal vocabulary words, and class vocabulary words.

Whatever your belief system about the best way to teach spelling and vocabulary, and whatever your preferred resources, they can easily be integrated into a regular Word-Work focus lesson.

It might be tempting to skip the 10 Steps to Teaching Independence for this final component of the Daily 5, but we still follow all the steps as we launch Word Work. It is especially important for students to understand the purpose so that the materials are viewed and used as tools for learning, not toys for passing time.

Figure 7.6
This student is happily engaged with Word Work using a small whiteboard and dry-erase marker.

Photo courtesy of Gelfand-Piper Photography.

The lesson begins like this: "Today we are going to learn about Word Work. It is important to spell words correctly when we write, because we care about our writing and the people who will read it. When we become better spellers, we become better readers and writers, plus . . . it's fun!"

We used to do Word Work for a whole round, but now we only do it for about ten minutes. We have learned that as the minutes tick by, the behavior of many students moves from a learning focus to a play focus, and stamina wanes. After ten minutes, we have students clean up and quietly move to their choice of Work on Writing or Read to Self.

As we create the I-chart for Word Work together, we note the differences between it and other Daily 5 choices.

As students model desired behaviors, then undesired and desired again, the following ideas are important for them to note and internalize:

- Quietly set up and clean up.
- Everyone who was using the materials helps to put them away.
- Materials go back in their tub, and the tub goes back to the same spot on the shelf.
- Leave materials neat, the way you would want to find them. This is respectful to our classmates.
- Get started quickly and quietly on Read to Self or Work on Writing after doing Word Work.

By the time our students have mastered Word Work, they have mastered the Daily 5. They now know everything they need to know about where materials are in the classroom, how we expect them to work independently whether alone or with a peer, and how to organize and monitor their time. And most important, this thoughtful, sustained, independent work in literacy has become a daily habit for them.

The Math Daily 3

The essence of mathematics is not to make simple things complicated but to make complicated things simple.

—Stanley Gudder

As you know, using the Daily 5 teaches our children to be independently engaged in meaningful literacy activities; it provides them with choice as well as the practice time needed to progress as readers. The structure allows us time to meet and confer with individuals and small groups, providing the focused one-on-one instruction needed to make optimal gains in literacy. Given the success of Daily 5 during literacy, we began to use the 10 Steps to Teaching and Learning Independence in almost everything we did.

We found ourselves using the steps to teach children how to be independent with science kits, with technology, with assuming correct hallway behaviors. The system even influenced our students' behavior at recess. One day we realized that our class had taken a piece of chart paper, tape, and markers outside to recess. There had been some trouble with tetherball, so the tetherball courts were off-limits for the day. The students posted the chart paper near the courts and created an I-chart for how to be independent when playing tetherball!

Since the Daily 5 was so successful, we began to wonder about its use in our math time. For us there always seemed to be a disconnect between our math and literacy blocks. In literacy we found our children making immense gains, as they had ample time to practice independently while we were able to work with small groups or individuals. The Daily 5 also provided the structure to deliver three or four shorter, whole-group focus lessons rather than one long whole-group lesson at the start of the literacy block. We were able to be certain our instruction reflected students' greatest needs. The literacy time in our room was our favorite time of the day—calm, engaging, and successful for our students.

Yet in math we were still struggling through each day with the whole-group "spray and pray" method of instruction we described in Chapter 2. You know, spray the children with a broad dose of whole-group instruction, not focused on the individual, specific needs of the children, and pray it works. Each day we found ourselves having to gear up to face math time as we delivered a whole-group lesson that was too long for students to stay engaged and that we knew was too challenging for many of our students and too easy for others. We always felt as though we had to strap on our running shoes and have an energy drink before math even began. We were in a constant state of racing around, supporting children who didn't understand the day's lesson and therefore could not work independently in their math book, as well as attempting to challenge others. What was it about math that made it so different from literacy?

In literacy, when we wanted to work with individuals and small groups, the rest of the class independently worked on reading and writing. This independent practice provided students the needed time to become better readers and writers. However, during math, when we worked with individuals or small groups, we had no idea what we should have the other children do. We used to have our students work in their math books for independent practice. But as with literacy workbooks, the math book didn't always provide the kind of mathematic problem solving and activities that would result in deeper understanding of the math concepts; nor did it keep the majority of our class engaged so we could successfully work with individuals and small groups. All this led us to develop the Math Daily 3.

Math Daily 3 is not about providing specific math content. It is about providing tasks and activities that engage students in the mathematics they are expected to learn (Van de Walle and Lovin 2006). This chapter is all about what we have our students do independently during math time. We follow the pattern of teaching independence for math time just as we do for the Daily 5 in literacy, leading to deeper mathematical understanding.

Since the beginning, Math Daily 3 has evolved. We began with Math Daily 5, patterning it after the five choices we were using in Daily 5 during literacy. We have since refined and established the Math Daily 3, which involves two or three rounds each day, depending on student stamina and the length of the math block. The Math Daily 3 are the following:

Math by Myself
Math Writing
Math with Someone

Both Math by Myself and Math with Someone are steeped in the kinesthetic practice of math concepts and are primarily activity based. These activities involve children in playing math games both alone and with partners as well as participating in activities and problem solving using manipulatives. At the beginning of a new math unit, the activities are mostly review and practice from prior units of study. This allows students to continue their practice of concepts already taught and helps them see that we don't forget one math concept just because we are introducing a new concept. However, as the new unit goes on, more of the Math Daily 3 activities become practice and reinforcement related to the current unit of study. Math by Myself and Math with Someone can also involve the use of computers or tablets as a means to independently practice strategies. There are also some activities and/or games that are fit for both Math by Myself and Math with Someone. Therefore these activities can have dual purpose.

Math Writing is the time students express and articulate their thinking and understanding by working on a particular math problem or math concept through pictures, numbers, and words, and occasionally by creating problems of their own as well.

Math Daily 3 Structure

The structure of Math Daily 3 (Figures 8.1 and 8.2) is very similar to that of the Daily 5. (See Figures 1.4 through 1.6 for the Daily 5 structure.)

Just as with the Daily 5, students with less stamina participate in three shorter rounds of Math Daily 3. For children with greater stamina, Math Daily 3 involves two longer rounds. We also find that the length of our math block can dictate whether or not we have time for two or three rounds of Math Daily 3.

Math Daily 3 provides a system to teach children to be independent with the math choices, using the 10 Steps to Independence, and provides a structure for the math block. As with the Daily 5, there are three bursts of

Figure 8.1
Primary structure of Math Daily 3, Three Rounds

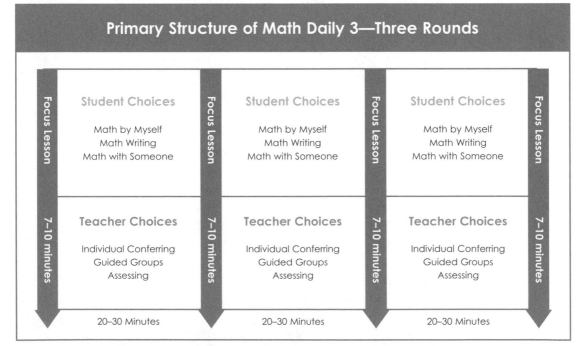

Primary Structure of Math Daily 3—Three Rounds

Focus Lesson 7–10 minutes	Student Choices Math by Myself Math Writing Math with Someone **Teacher Choices** Individual Conferring Guided Groups Assessing	Focus Lesson 7–10 minutes	Student Choices Math by Myself Math Writing Math with Someone **Teacher Choices** Individual Conferring Guided Groups Assessing	Focus Lesson 7–10 minutes	Student Choices Math by Myself Math Writing Math with Someone **Teacher Choices** Individual Conferring Guided Groups Assessing	Focus Lesson 7–10 minutes
	20–30 Minutes		20–30 Minutes		20–30 Minutes	

Figure 8.2
Intermediate
structure of
Math Daily 3,
Two Rounds

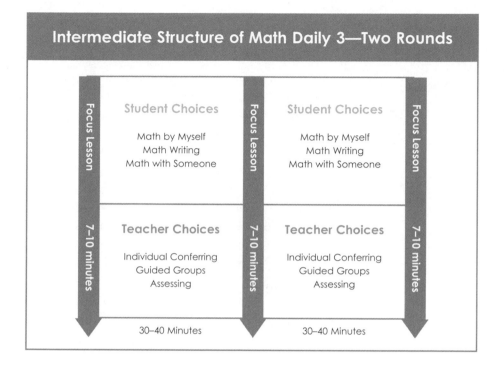

instruction and two or three independent work times, and we typically wrap up Math Daily 3 with sharing and review of what we learned that day.

We obtain the whole-group lessons for short bursts of mathematical instruction from our school's math program. As with literacy, we look at each lesson with a discerning eye. Many of the math lessons from a math textbook are not brain compatible, having lessons that run too long. (See "Brain Research," page 28.) Therefore, before teaching any lesson, we decide which part of the lesson is important and necessary and what can be eliminated in order to most effectively teach the concept to the group of children we have. The necessary components of the whole-group lesson for that day are broken into manageable chunks to be taught during the whole-group focus lessons, which take place between rounds of Math Daily 3. This allows for us to craft the length of the lessons much closer to a brain-compatible time, enhancing the opportunity for children to retain the learning and information (Figure 8.1).

Math lessons always have plenty of student participation. Combining the brain research of short focus lessons with the gradual release of responsibility, the first focus lesson in Math Daily 3 is the explicit teaching of a math concept. The second lesson allows students more time for guided practice of the same concept. The third lesson is often a problem that reflects the lesson focus for the day. Students work on this problem either independently or with an elbow buddy. They share their thinking and strategy either with a partner or as a whole group, which allows students to collaborate and problem solve together through the use of manipulatives, turn-and-talk, sharing, and practice. Figure 8.3 is an example of a math lesson that shows how the gradual release of responsibility is used as we teach each focus lesson centered on one math concept during Math Daily 3.

We also keep in mind the gradual release of responsibility during each short lesson. In the past we would teach one lengthy, whole-group lesson and give an assignment, and if students didn't grasp the concept, we would race around and do our best to reteach, support, and challenge, all in the very short time left over after the long whole-group lesson. Our instruction went directly from the "I show you" to the "you do it" stages of release, not allowing for guided practice, and we must admit, this approach was not terribly successful, in particular with our more at-risk math students. Now each day our focus lessons generally follow the gradual release of responsibility model, I do, we do, you do, which allows for more modeling and guided practice for students. As Fisher and Frey (2008) state, "We must transfer responsibility for learning to our students gradually—and offer support at every step" (32).

Math Daily 3 Overview

We begin our math block with the first Math Daily 3 focus lesson (Figure 8.4), which we design from a concept or lesson in our math curriculum. This first lesson is the introduction and teaching of the concept for the day. The instruction during this lesson is focused on modeling, thinking out loud, and directly teaching the concept while students observe and follow along, often with the use of manipulatives, whiteboards, and so on.

Once the first focus lesson is complete, we let the class know whom we are going to be meeting with in a small group, and the rest of the students check in with their first choice of the Math Daily 3. (See "Check-In," page 111.)

While students participate independently in their Math Daily 3 choices, we work with the small group, again making sure the lesson length coincides with the brain research. This small group is often composed of students who need more support with the lesson taught, may benefit from

Sample Lessons Using the Gradual Release Model

	Today's Lesson
CCSS	Operations & Algebraic Thinking, Grades 1–4 (many specific standards fit this lesson)
Focus Lesson 1 (I do)	*"A product is the result or answer when you multiply two numbers together. Today we are going to learn how to use a number line to help us find a product when we multiply."*
	"Starting at 0, and skipping five numbers each time, I want to know how many skips it takes to get to the number 20." Using the whiteboard, document camera, or projector, display a number line and model with a counter or pointer how many skips of five can be taken on the number line to get to the number 20. Think aloud as you do this. Introduce the equation 5 x 4 = 20. Explain to students, *"Starting at 0, I was able to skip four times to land on the 20."*
	Encourage the children to count aloud with you as you do the same problem again.
	Round of Math Daily 3
Focus Lesson 2 (We do)	*"Who can tell me what the product of a multiplication problem is?* [Students respond.] *Yes! The product is the answer! Earlier I modeled for you how to use a number line to find the product when multiplying. Now we are going to practice this together."*
	Use a large class number line with a pointer and call on various students to model as you present problems. The whole class would be encouraged to count along with the student using the pointer. Class discussion should take place and a variety of problems should be answered together.
	Be sure to use small and large numbers as factors. After a few problems, encourage students to predict the products ahead of time and then confirm their answer by skip-counting using the number line.
	Round of Math Daily 3
Focus Lesson 3 (You do)	Give each child a counter, a number line, and a piece of paper. Ask students to create a problem to trade with a friend. Students will trade problems and use the number line to solve the problem they are given. After doing this, have a class discussion in which children use the number line in their description of how they solved the problem.
	Ask children, *"I am a number between 21 and 25. You say my name when you skip by fours. What number am I?"* Encourage children to share how they solved this problem. You may wish to have children create problems similar to this and trade with friends as well (depending on time and perceived student understanding).
	Student Sharing

Figure 8.3   This lesson was adapted from http://illuminations.nctm.org/LessonDetail.aspx?ID=L316.

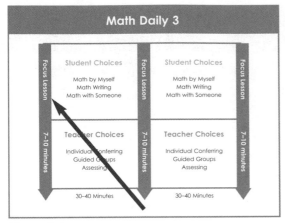

Figure 8.4
The arrow indicates the location of the first focus lesson within the Math Daily 3 structure.

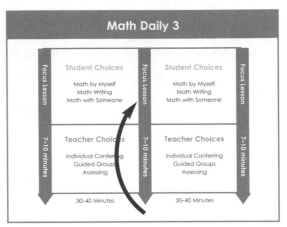

Figure 8.5
The arrow indicates the location of the second focus lesson in the Math Daily 3 structure.

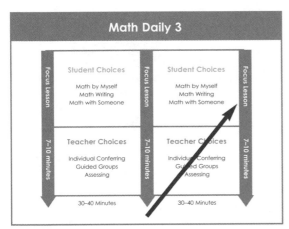

Figure 8.6
The arrow indicates the final whole-group focus lesson and wrap-up of the concept taught that day.

preteaching the next portion of the lesson, or may need to review yesterday's lesson for maximum understanding. By pulling them together we are able to reinforce the lesson and concept. At the completion of the small-group work, students check in with one of the Math Daily 3 choices, and we hop up and begin our individual conferences. Between each conference, we glance about the room, checking for student stamina. Once we see that stamina is breaking down, we call the group back to the gathering place for the second whole-group lesson.

The second whole-group short burst of instruction (Figure 8.5) involves continuing the first lesson, with students participating in the lesson's concept through the gradual release stage of "we do it." This lesson engages students in guided practice of the concept through the continued use of math manipulatives, paper, whiteboards, or a variety of other materials. At the conclusion of this second lesson, students check in and begin a second round of the Math Daily 3. As before, while students are engaged in their math choices, we work with a small group of students. When their lesson is complete, they check in with their Math Daily 3 choice and we continue with individual conferring.

After the second practice time, the third short burst of instruction involves "you do it." This is when students practice on their own or with a partner. We like to keep students in the gathering place or nearby, with us sitting right there to nudge, guide, and support as necessary. During each whole-group instruction time we monitor and note which child or children may need extra support or practice with the concept, as those are the students we need to either meet with in a small group or confer with individually. The last focus lesson involves reviewing the concept taught and students sharing their strategies (Figure 8.6).

What Do You Need to Begin Math Daily 3?

Similar to the Daily 5, the Math Daily 3 requires wall space on which to build the Math Daily 3 board (Figure 8.7) and to post the I-charts. The Math Daily 3 board organizes each of the independent math activities under the categories of Math by Myself, Math Writing, and Math with Someone.

In order to keep students' confusion at bay, our math gathering space is in a different location from the literacy space. It is here that we house the

Figure 8.7
The building of a Math Daily 3 board, located in a different spot from the Daily 5 area.

I-charts, Math Daily 3 board, chart rack, overhead projector, document camera, and interactive whiteboard.

Math Daily 3 requires many materials. These materials most likely will include manipulatives, game pieces, dice, cards, game boards, small whiteboards, game markers, and so on. And there are numerous ways to organize these materials. We have found that the organizational method of the materials is very individual to each teacher's style. Much like the difference between using a notebook for Work on Writing and using a folder holding loose paper, teachers often feel passionate about their preferred materials and method for organizing them. What matters most is that the teacher can manage the organizational method and teach students to do so as well.

That said, we have some strategies that have helped us greatly in managing the myriad materials required to support student independence with Math Daily 3.

Game Boards

Many of the math games and independent activities require a game board. There are many ways in which we have organized these boards that allow for students to be independent in obtaining the board, using it, and putting it away. We found our friend Allison's idea to be one of the most successful. Each time a board is required, we create it on 8.5-by-11-inch paper and place it in a clear plastic slip-in binder sheet. The sheets are then added to a binder, which is located in a place where students can easily access it. (If no plastic sheets are available, each board can also be hole-punched and put in the binder.) One of the great advantages to this organizational method is that game boards can be placed into two sections within each binder—Math by Myself and Math with Someone—with a divider sheet between them, making it quick and easy to find the right game board. The other reason this method works so well is that multiple binders with the same game boards can be on hand. Having many binders in the room means that no one has to wait for a game board. Finally, depending on students' needs to practice certain concepts, game boards can be removed or replaced.

Dice, Game Board Counters, and Cards

Keeping all the tiny little pieces for counters, game boards, dice, and of course cards organized and simple to set up and clean up can make or break Math Daily 3. We have found there are two primary ways to manage this.

One way is to create a "tool kit" for each child. For us the tool kit is merely a zippered plastic bag with a number on it. Each child is assigned to a specific number and chooses that bag each day. The bags are stored in tubs, and each tub is labeled with which bags are contained inside. About ten bags fit in each tub. This management structure expedites locating the individual bags. Each bag contains all the components needed for participation in Math by Myself and Math with Someone: game pieces, dice, decks of cards, counters, and so on. We found that when using this organizational method for the math materials, it's helpful to put the corresponding bag number on every item that goes into the bag. That way, when an errant piece is found it's easy to locate the tub that holds the bag and return it to its proper place.

The obvious downside to the tool-kit method of organizing math materials is that classrooms need to have enough materials for each child's bag. The other challenge this system presents is the time required for gathering and labeling each little piece with the corresponding bag number.

Another option for organizing all of the required materials for Math Daily 3 is to put materials in containers, which children gather according to their particular needs.

Figure 8.8 shows a simple and effective way to store and make available the small counters and pieces for Math Daily 3. It is merely a plastic

Figure 8.8
A multi-drawer plastic storage bin, found at many hardware stores, works well for organizing the many small materials needed for Math Daily 3.

case found at any home improvement store; it typically is used to hold small nails, nuts, and bolts. In each drawer we place counters, markers, and so on. When children need these items, they simply remove the small drawer and take it to their work area. The drawer is easy to use and then return at the end of each round of Math Daily 3. Oftentimes we glue the type of material on the outside of the drawer, expediting the return of loose materials to the correct place.

Decks of cards, a variety of types of dice, and other items too large to store in the small drawers are contained in a plastic rolling cart with drawers (Figure 8.9). This allows for easy organization of the materials and for them to be moved about the room to a place that is easy to access during Math Daily 3.

Math Tools by Unit of Study

Many units of study, such as measurement, geometry, and operations, require content-specific tools. These tools are also housed in either the individual tool kits or community gathering places like those we described in the preceding section.

Figure 8.9
A rolling cart with drawers houses larger math materials needed to participate in Math Daily 3 activities.

Other Math Daily 3 Supply Staples

Student math notebooks or journals are housed in social-group tubs (Figure 8.10); children are assigned to a tub, where their materials are held. (It is not a tub of like-level students or specifically assigned groups.) The tubs allow for a more efficient use of space in our rooms; if we had a desk and chair for every student in the room, where they could store their individual supplies, we would not have enough room for a gathering place, a small-group work area, and individual and partner group spots (see more about classroom design on our website, www.thedailycafe.com).

Individual whiteboards are a staple for Math Daily 3. Whiteboards provide children with a way to show their thinking in whole and small groups, to record ideas, and to work on problem solving. Yet housing whiteboards can be tricky. Some years we place individual whiteboards in the student social-group tubs. This way our students can quickly get their whiteboards and whiteboard crayons and erasers from small, group tubs rather than congregating to get these materials from a whole-group location.

Figure 8.10 Student notebooks and journals are housed in social-group tubs.

The downside to this method is that the boards often become scratched or worn due to the heavy daily use of getting things in and out of the tub. However, Solo plastic plates are a wonderful and less expensive option, and the local hardware stores are willing to cut shower board to fit nicely into any size tub.

We have also housed the whiteboards in stacks around the room, making them ready for children to grab. The whiteboard crayons are then housed in a bin near the boards, where they are placed individually into a clean sock that is used as an eraser. By placing the writing tool in the sock students can quickly and easily grab a sock rather than have to juggle the board, crayon, and eraser all at once.

Teaching the Foundation Lessons of Math Daily 3

The Math Daily 3 foundation lessons are essentially the same as the relevant Daily 5 foundation lessons, so just as with the Daily 5, we begin foundation lessons for Math Daily 3 on the first day of school. The first foundation lesson involves instructing children how to gather materials, build stamina for working with a math game independently, and correctly replace the materials. Being that much of the Math Daily 3 choices involve materials and games, teaching children to be independent with the use of these materials is vital.

We begin teaching building stamina as well as setting up and cleaning up the materials through basic Math by Myself activities, taken from our math program, from online sites, from books, and so on. You can find games we use on our website, www.thedailycafe.com, under Math Daily 3. This portion of the site is expanding weekly. Math games can support the practice of the mathematical concepts we are teaching and can be useful in reviewing concepts from the previous year. Working together as a staff to pass along favorite math games to the other teachers is a helpful way to start the year.

Launching Math by Myself

Once we've chosen a Math-by-Myself activity to teach to the group, we begin by modeling where the materials are located, how to gather them, and how to play the game or participate in the activity. We make certain it is simple and quick to teach. This is why it is often helpful for the first Math-by-Myself activity to be one the class may know from last year.

Figure 8.11
Once a math
activity is taught,
it is written on a
sentence strip
and posted on
the Math Daily 3
wall under the
correct heading.

Once it is taught, we write the name of the game or activity on a short sentence strip and post it under the Math-by-Myself heading on our Math Daily 3 board (Figure 8.11). For many activities, we draw a quick, rudimentary picture of the supplies needed right on the sentence strip label. This will help children be completely independent; when they choose that activity, they won't need to ask anyone what supplies to gather.

Once the activity is taught, we begin the 10 Steps to Independence for Math by Myself. The I-chart we create with steps 1, 2, and 3 generally follows the pattern of the Daily 5.

Step 1. Identify what is to be taught: Math by Myself

Step 2. Set a purpose and create a sense of urgency: It is a great way to become better at math and it is fun!

Step 3. Record desired behaviors of Math by Myself on an I-chart (Figure 8.12): This is where Math Daily 3 I-chart varies slightly. Since it is the first day, we put four items on the I-chart:

    Set up materials quickly and quietly

    Get started right away

    Stay in one spot

    Work on math the whole time

Step 4. Model most-desirable behaviors: We have one or two children model picking up the materials and getting ready to play. While

Figure 8.12
Math by Myself
I-Chart

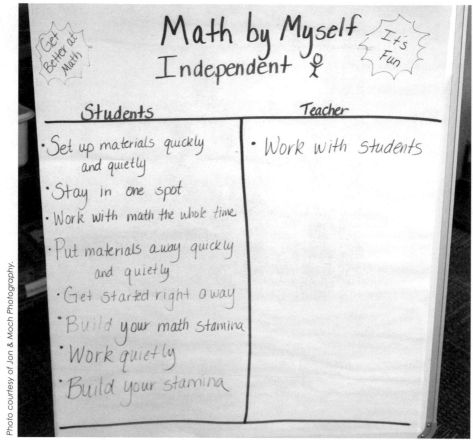

Photo courtesy of Jon & Moch Photography.

they stay in one spot and play the game, we stand by the I-chart and ask the group to look at the student(s) modeling. "Did they gather the materials quickly and quietly? Are they staying in one spot? Are they working the whole time?" The class answers yes, and then the next question is asked, similar to that of the Daily 5: "Will they become better at math if they exhibit these behaviors?" Yes! The student(s) then model putting the materials away in the right spot, quickly and quietly.

Step 5. Model least-desirable behaviors, then most-desirable behaviors again: Just as in the Daily 5, we choose a student who might be likely to exhibit undesirable behaviors. As the student gathers materials, he or she doesn't get set up or work the whole time, and so on. We stand by the I-chart and ask about the behaviors. This time the class answers no when asked if the student gathered materials quickly and quietly, is working the whole time, and is staying in one spot. Of course, the vital question, "Will he or she become better at math if they act this way?" is answered with a resounding no! We then ask the student modeling to change his or her behavior and model correctly.

Step 6. Place students around the room. We call small groups of students to gather their materials, and we quickly send them to a variety of places around the room, just as in the Daily 5.

Step 7. Practice and build stamina: Again, we allow everyone to practice by themselves and build their stamina.

Step 8. Stay out of the way: While students are practicing, we stay out of the way so they learn to work by themselves, without us. Even though we are not looking at or speaking to the students, we are very aware of when the first person runs out of stamina.

Step 9. Use a quiet signal to bring students back to the gathering place: As soon as the first person loses stamina, we call everyone back to the group. On their way, they put materials away correctly, quietly, and quickly.

Step 10. Conduct a group check-in; ask, "How did it go?": As with the Daily 5, we have our students show one, two, three, or four fingers to indicate how they did with each of the items on the I-chart.

After we have gone through the 10 Steps to Independence once, including a practice round on their own, we have a decision to make. Do our students have enough focus to go through the 10 Steps again with the same game, adding to the I-chart and building stamina? Or are they done for the time being? Either way, the next time we go through the 10 Steps to Independence, we will add one of the next student behaviors:

Get started right away
Build math stamina
Work quietly

Each day as we are getting Math Daily 3 up and running, we either review the Math-by-Myself activity from the first day or introduce a new Math-by-Myself activity, depending on the needs of the class. We continue to add the independent behaviors to the I-chart and add Math-by-Myself activities to the Math Daily 3 board.

Teaching the Foundation Lessons: Math Writing

▪ ▪ ▪ ▪ ▪ Student stamina is short at the beginning of the year, when we're launching Math by Myself. The question arises, "What do we do for the rest of our math block?" As with the Daily 5 for literacy, we use the rest of the Math block to teach the foundation lessons for Math Writing and Math with Someone. As we mentioned, Math Writing is the time students express their thinking and understanding of a math concept or problem solve through pictures, numbers, and words. We gather Math Writing activities from a variety of places: our math curriculum and problem-solving concepts, story problems that coincide with the current math concept being taught, and a Problem of the Day. All of these resources are available in our own math programs, books, and online. We provide many activities on our website, www.thedailycafe.com, under Math Daily 3.

After we teach and students practice each activity for Math Writing, we fill out a sentence strip label for the activity and add it to the Math Daily 3 board.

Each day after students participate in Math by Myself and build stamina, we do a whole-group lesson on one of the Math Writing problems or activities. The goal, as in the Daily 5, is to teach the activities and have children practice so that by the time we launch Math Writing, they will be able to participate in the activity independently and with stamina.

Launching Math Writing

▪ ▪ ▪ ▪ ▪ Once our students have built their stamina with Math by Myself (see page 106 for number of optimal minutes of stamina before introducing the next Daily 5), we launch Math Writing. Through the use of the 10 Steps to Independence, the I-chart is built slowly, starting with the first two independent behaviors listed here:

> Stay in one spot
> Work on Math Writing the whole time
> Get started right away
> Build math stamina
> Work quietly

Once Math by Myself and Math Writing are up and running for the desired minutes, we introduce choice. It is introduced exactly like it is for the Daily 5 in literacy (see page 110). Students participate in two rounds of Math Daily 3 practice, choosing either Math by Myself or Math Writing to do first and the other to do second. This practice of choosing between two of the Math Daily 3 components lasts for three to four days before we launch Math with Someone.

Launching Math with Someone

While we are building stamina for Math by Myself and Math Writing, we are also teaching foundation lessons during the Daily 5 in literacy. One of the important foundation lessons in the Daily 5 that will need to be taught to support Math Daily 3 is How to Choose a Partner (see page 98).

When students have built their stamina for Math by Myself and Math Writing to the number of minutes we consider appropriate before adding the next Math Daily 3 choice (see page 106), and once students have been introduced to and practiced How to Choose a Partner during literacy in the Daily 5, we are ready to introduce Math with Someone.

The first day of Math with Someone looks very similar to the first day of Math by Myself (see page 134). We begin by teaching an activity that requires partners. During the teaching of the activity, we also model getting materials and cleaning up the materials even though the students are accustomed to this protocol through Math with Myself. Again, our activities come from a variety of places—math curriculum, online, professional books, and our website. After we teach the activity, we add the sentence strip activity label, which includes required materials, to the Math Daily 3 board.

As soon as the activity has been introduced and written on the Math Daily 3 board, we begin the 10 Steps to Independence. At this point many of the students will see the correlation between this I-chart and the others used in math and literacy. Therefore, we often are able to put all of the desired behaviors on the I-chart right away rather than begin with just two:

Set up materials quickly and quietly
Stay in one spot
Work on math the whole time
Put materials away in the correct spot, quickly and quietly
Get started right away
Build math stamina
Work quietly

Building stamina and introducing a variety of Math-with-Someone activities follows the same pattern as Math by Myself. If we find that the noise level is too high, we limit the number of partnerships who participate each round until everyone has a turn, instead of everyone working in partners at the same time.

■   ■   ■

The Math Daily 3, just as the Daily 5, has changed our math instruction and the resulting outcomes with students. Since our students now work independently on activities that allow for the practice of current math concepts and review of past concepts, we are able to work closely with children individually and in small groups consistently each day. This individualized coaching allows our students to receive tailored instruction to best meet their needs. Focused math instruction coupled with independent practice has our children experiencing more success with math than ever before and has created a culture of learning similar to the Daily 5 time that we love. We no longer dread math time, but look forward to the calm, engaging, and joyful work experienced by both our students and us.

Returning to Our Core Beliefs

Do what you can, with what you have, where you are.
—Theodore Roosevelt

At this juncture, we want to address how we handle parent volunteers, guest teachers, new students, and the most challenging students in the room. These can be tricky to manage and have the ability to enhance or detract from the classroom culture we work so hard to build. We deal with each one firmly grounded in our core beliefs of community, accountability, trust, and respect.

Barometer Children

Barometer child is a term we lovingly give to the child or children who dictate the weather in the classroom (see page 48).

It is important not only for the individual barometer child or children but also for the whole classroom community that the teacher finds effective ways to support the barometer child. We absolutely trust and believe that with appropriate support from us as the teachers, the barometer children will be successful in our classrooms. It is a self-fulfilling prophecy; children will rise to the expectations we set for them.

When first launching the Daily 5, if the same student or students are responsible for the break in stamina for three to five days in a row, we move into action, putting a series of one to four levels of support into place as needed (Figure 9.1).

Level 1: Reflection

The first and most important level of support for barometer students is our own reflection. It's very easy to blame our students for a lack of stamina, but if we have skipped any of the 10 Steps to Independence, then the failure is more rightfully placed on our shoulders. We may have been tempted to skip the most-desirable and least-desirable modeling portions of the 10 Steps, yet upon reflection we may realize that students did indeed need to see the expectations clearly modeled. We may also discover upon reflection that we have been engaging with the barometer child instead of staying out of the way. These students often find attention for negative behavior as desirable as attention for positive.

One thing we check right away are the books in these students' book boxes. Are they a good fit? Do these students like them and find them engaging? We are vigilant with these students in helping them choose more good-fit books as soon as they are done with those in their book box.

Levels of Support for Barometer Children

Level 1: Reflection

The teacher reflects on their own teaching practice:
1. Did I teach the 10 steps to Independence explicitly?
2. Am I visually keeping my eyes and body away from the barometer child?
3. Do I continually use a repectful voice level and tone (no sharp tongue)?
4. Remember that deposits must be made before withdrawal.
5. Chart teacher deposits.

Level 2: Extra Support

1. Student stays in during recess for 2–3 minutes practicing most desirable behavior.
2. Student continues to practice during recess for 3–5 days until behavior starts to change.
If independent behavior is not improving, move to level 3.

Tracking Positive Behaviors

9–10	10–11	11–12	12–1	1–2	2–3

Level 3: In-Class Modifications

1. Square yard of fabric, 2 sand timers, book box, small bag of manipulatives (e.g., Legos, play dough, different reading materials)
Teach student to work with body on fabric, using the sand timer, alternating between reading and manipulation of things.

Level 4: Gradual Release of In-Class Modifications

Sandwich—When conferring, check on barometer child first, then move to a different student, return to barometer child for a quick check-in, move to another student, etc. Sandwich support for our barometer children between our support for other children.

Figure 9.1
A series of levels of support is put into place as needed for barometer children.

Sometimes these students come to us depleted of positive interactions. Therefore, we are especially careful when working with barometer students to continue using nothing but a positive tone of voice so that, as Stephen Covey (1989) put it, we fill up their emotional bank account before any withdrawals are taken. Tone of voice is essential, along with noticing the positive and appropriate behaviors of these students throughout the day. To do this, we often put ourselves on a "plan." This merely involves using a visual in the form of a sheet of paper on which the day is divided into hours and hours into smaller segments. We tuck this visual into our conferring notebook or laptop, where it serves as a visual reminder to observe and give the barometer student feedback for positive behaviors and interactions (Figure 9.2).

Figure 9.2
As you can see from this example, we were running out of steam with this student by the end of the day. It became clear to us that we needed to ask colleagues for support. Identifying other people to periodically pop into our room during our most difficult hours to offer positive support to our barometer children lets them know that others in the school notice their positive attributes as well, not just their classroom teacher. Working together as a team and surrounding our barometer children with adults who support them is one of the greatest gifts we can give our most at-risk students.

My Plan					
9–10	10–11	11–12	12–1	1–2	2–3
✓	✓	✓	✓	✓	✓
✓	✓	✓	✓	✓	
✓	✓	✓	✓	✓	
✓		✓			

Before we move on to the other levels of support, we make sure that the limited stamina exhibited by the class is not a result of our action or inaction. A trusted colleague who is willing to observe our behaviors can often help us see the issue at hand.

If we can identify for a fact that we have successfully implemented all of the items listed for level 1 to support our barometer students and the behaviors are still present, we move to level 2.

Level 2: Extra Support

If the same child is the first person to lose stamina for a few days in a row, and we have thoroughly reflected on our teaching practice for level 1, we know it is time to provide extra support.

For this support, we privately and kindly ask the barometer child to join us at recess so they can practice building their stamina. When the barometer child stays in from recess to practice, that is exactly what they do, practice, but only for two or three minutes (goodness—they are typically the students who need to be outside the most!). We have the student tell us why he or she is there and, if necessary (and continuing with the kind tone of voice), we share that they are there to practice the behaviors of independence for Read to Self, or any other Daily 5. We then explicitly label the behavior or behaviors. For example, we might say, "Jake, I noticed you had a difficult time staying in one spot. Go ahead and get your book box and go read over there, and work on building your stamina for staying in one spot."

After the child is set up, we move out of their way to let them practice on their own. At the end of a few minutes, we stop the student and, using the I-chart, review what he or she just did and let the student know that we are certain he or she will be able to be successful tomorrow. If the student struggles again the next day, we practice again at recess.

If necessary, we continue to keep the student in from recess for three to five days, watching to see if this level of support helps change the behavior. This level of support is sufficient for the majority of our barometer students. One benefit of this is that it helps us determine if a child's behavior challenges are to seek attention or if something more organic (beyond their control) is at the root of the behavioral challenge. Often after a few days of staying in at recess to practice, the behavior will change. This shows us that the child is more of an attention-based behavior student and has tired of missing recess and not getting much attention at all from us. If we see absolutely no change, we are aware that this child may not be able to control his or her behaviors, which means we need to go to the next level of support.

Level 3: In-Class Modifications

If we have determined that a student needs more support than level 2 provides, we move into offering a variety of in-class modifications. These modifications help barometer students build stamina at their own rate, which appears to be a different pace from that of the rest of the class. We begin by gathering tools that we have found can help students build their stamina to become independent, which include square yards of different colors and textures of fabric or moveable small rugs. We can also create "offices," which are rectangular shapes outlined on the floor with tape or chalk. One student even found success by sitting in a laundry basket to do Read to Self. He just needed the security and solidity of the basket around him in order to focus. (See Figures 9.3a and 9.3b.) Other tools we gather are sand timers of varying lengths of time or stopwatches. We also collect kinesthetic materials, such as play dough, a small bag of pattern blocks, Legos, and other manipulatives (Figure 9.4). After we teach a short, whole-group focus lesson and everyone checks in, we explain to the barometer child that we are going to help him or her build stamina. To begin with, we will work on staying in one spot. We ask the barometer student to choose

Figure 9.3a
The in-class modification for this child? A laundry basket "office." He loved it, and it worked.

Figure 9.3b
We sometimes mark office boundaries on the floor with masking tape or chalk.

Figure 9.4
Students make
use of
kinesthetic
materials during
their lessons.

Photo courtesy of Gelfand-Piper Photography.

a place to set up: a piece of fabric to sit on that feels good to them, which we help place in an appropriate location, or one of the "offices." These spaces offer extra visual—sometimes even physical—support to our more kinesthetic children, which greatly helps them stay in one spot.

After we help the student settle into place, we talk with him or her about staying in one spot and reading the whole time. Since the barometer child has shown the inability to focus and sustain reading we provide a second tool, a sand timer, which gives a visual cue of how long the child must push themselves to read without stopping. Third, we provide one of the manipulatives, ideally something he or she enjoys or has shown interest in. We teach the barometer child to flip over the timer, read until the sand runs out, flip the timer over again, work with the manipulative until the sand runs out, flip the timer again, read again, and so on. The manipulatives provide a kinesthetic, but quiet, brain break for the child, and he or she gets back to reading after a minute, practicing the behaviors correctly. We know that many of you are thinking, "But you don't know my barometer students. There is no way they will put the manipulatives away when the sand runs out." That may be correct, but at the beginning, our first step is to get them to stay in one place. We will continue to support them with the reading as time goes on.

For older children who are able to manage a stopwatch, we make some adjustments. They time themselves when they start reading and then stop

Figure 9.5
A "barometer
student"
recorded her
stamina for
reading and the
time spent using
manipulatives so
she could see
and be
encouraged by
her progress
over time.

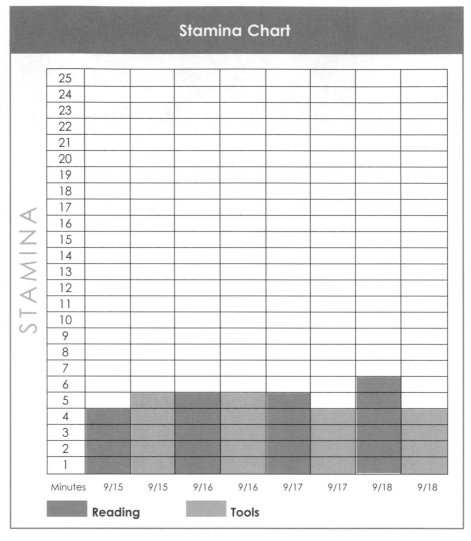

timing when their stamina breaks down. On a stamina chart, they record the date and the number of minutes they were able to sustain reading (Figure 9.5). Beginning the stopwatch again, they use the kinesthetic manipulatives for a brain break. Instead of manipulatives, older students may prefer materials like I Spy books, world record books by Guinness, and joke books. They graph the number of minutes needed for the brain break on the same chart.

The goal of this type of in-class modification is twofold. We want to take the longer work time the rest of the class is participating in and break it down for the barometer student so that it is in more manageable chunks of time and those chunks are coupled with brain breaks. This gives students who build stamina more slowly tools to assist them. The other goal is to allow the rest of the class uninterrupted time to continue building their own stamina.

When the barometer child has mastered this time goal with the first sand timer (or stopwatch goal we set with an older student), we introduce a second, longer timer. We mark the new timer with a B, for book, and the original, shorter timer continues to be the manipulative timer. We practice with the student as they flip over the B timer while reading, and then flip over the first timer while taking a brain break. The student continues to practice with the timers until we see the ability to sustain independence with the new, longer timer. Then we substitute the B timer with an even longer timer. By slowly increasing the length of time the barometer child is reading, interspersed with kinesthetic brain breaks, they are able to build stamina at a pace that works best for them.

With our older students, we hold a daily conference at the beginning of Daily 5 or, if needed, at the start of each round of Daily 5. In these short conversations we review their stamina charts, talking about what is working and what isn't and helping them set a goal for the day. At the end of each round or at the end of Daily 5 we do a quick check-in to see how it went.

If students are struggling with letting go of the manipulatives or alternative reading material when the brain break timer runs out, we have a variety of other strategies to support these students.

The first course of action is to once again check the books in their book boxes to make certain they are a good fit and are engaging. Another strategy is to periodically use proximity to the student when the class is practicing building their stamina. We stand close but do not look at or engage with them. When the brain break time lapses, they are more inclined to move back to reading if they know we are close by. With students who are very challenged with staying in one spot as well as returning to reading when the sand runs out, we bring in a timer that makes a single, short tone when it goes off. We place the timer a short distance away from the location of the child, along with the manipulatives or alternative reading. When the timer sounds at the end of the brain break, the barometer student gets up, puts the manipulatives next to the timer, resets the timer, and returns to his or her spot. This gets the student up a bit, providing what may be much-needed movement as well as removing the manipulatives from his or her reach while reading. At first the class may look up when the timer goes off, but they will soon ignore it as just one of the many background noises in all classrooms.

On the same note, with students who need even more movement, we place the manipulatives and timer outside the classroom door. With this strategy, they go outside to get the manipulatives and reset the timer. This provides the physical movement their bodies need without disturbing the rest of the class by moving within the room.

It is not uncommon for other children to want to have a piece of fabric or manipulatives as well. We explain that these are simply tools, and although anyone is welcome to use a square of fabric or one of the empty "offices," the other tools are reserved for people who have a different plan to help them reach their goals.

We've found that once stamina is developed, barometer children outgrow their need for the items and willingly give them up. It is always our desire to have children be able to participate in Daily 5 without tools, so we work individually with each child to find the best time for that, knowing they can always return to the tools if necessary. We have even had students who come in on a particularly challenging day and ask for the tools themselves.

Level 4: Gradual Release of In-Class Modifications

There will be times when our most challenging students will need extra support from us, even after they have moved away from using the tools. We call this fourth level of support Gradual Release of In-Class Modifications. Simply stated, this method involves "sandwiching" quick check-ins with a child during a Daily 5 round. Once we have completed a whole-group lesson, small guided group, or individual conference, we quietly walk by the barometer child and do a quick check-in, asking them how it's going and offering a word of encouragement or a bit of support. This is done on the way to another individual conference. At the end of the other conference, we swing by our barometer child again, doing a check-in similar to the first. We continue this process during the whole round of Daily 5.

The act of sandwiching a quick check-in between small-group and individual instruction gives the child just enough support to help them be considerably more successful than they would be if we expected them to do a complete round of Daily 5 independently. Level 4 support for our barometer children is just one of the reasons we no longer sit at a table or on the floor and call students over to us. We use that "walking-to-my-next-conference" time to respectfully and subtly offer proactive support to our most at-risk students.

In Chapter 2 we wrote: "Trusting children is the underpinning of what makes the Daily 5 work. Trust is believing the best of others, even if actions or behaviors seem incongruent." We know that it can be slow and challenging to help that barometer child achieve the degree of stamina needed to help him or her gain the amount of practice time needed to become a better reader and writer. But stick with it, and trust that with your support it will happen.

Guest Teachers

If the barometer child creates the weather in the classroom, a guest teacher might represent an unexpected front that comes through from time to time. There are several things we can do to support the guest teacher and help him or her maintain the predictable schedule to which our students are accustomed and on which their success depends.

We love the children whom we teach. We strive to make each moment with them meaningful, worthwhile, and productive. We also want their time with a guest teacher to be as valuable. Handing off the teaching to someone else is time consuming at best; writing lesson plans that are detailed enough that learning continues at a high level, explaining the schedules and the nuances for each child, accounting for the behaviors that may change in our absence—all require a great deal of effort. Yet addressing the needs of our students and setting the stage for everyone's success is rooted in maintaining a schedule to which the students are accustomed.

We write a generic lesson plan explaining the Daily 5 and save it on our computer. In that way, much of the work of explaining the schedule and structure of the literacy block is already in place. This makes our job of writing lesson plans much easier, but, more important, it maintains the high level of learning that needs to take place whether we are the teacher or we have a guest teacher. The sample guest teacher plans that follow are also in Appendix G.

Sample Guest Teacher Plans

Welcome! Thanks so much for coming! This wonderful group of children responds very well to kind, positive words. They are very independent and know the routines well, so I'm sure your day will run smoothly. Don't hesitate to honor them by following their lead; they are a great group.

Schedule at a Glance

> 8:40–8:55 Students enter the classroom when they arrive at school (open campus) and begin book shopping.
>
> 8:55 School starts: attendance, welcome, etc.
>
> 9:00–9:15 Calendar
>
> 9:15–11:50 Daily 5 and writing workshop
>
> 11:50–12:50 Lunch and recess
>
> 12:50–2:00 Math
>
> 2:00–2:30 Third block (Flex Block: Science/SS, Handwriting, Art)
>
> 2:30–2:50 Recess
>
> 2:50–3:20 Chapter book
>
> 3:20 Dismissal

Students will begin coming into the room about 8:40 or whenever they arrive at school. Please remind them to (1) order lunch, (2) check in on the Daily Graph, (3) grab their book boxes, (4) read or shop for "good-fit books." They will do this until the bell rings at 8:55.

8:55 Day begins: Ask helpers to count up lunches. You will record lunches and absent students on the attendance report, which is in the blue folder. Helpers will take this report to the office. The daily helpers will assist you throughout the day.

Review the schedule with students. Ask if they can make a true statement about the Daily Graph.

Stand and recite the flag salute, and then have the helpers lead the class over to the math calendar.

9:00 Calendar: The helpers will begin leading the calendar. You act as a participant as the helpers manage and run the calendar time.

Move into shared reading on the carpet: Today's literature selection is _____. We are working on modeling fluency as well as the strategy Back Up and Reread as a way to fix up Check for Understanding if and when comprehension breaks down or when a word is read incorrectly.

Daily 5

Here is the structure of Daily 5:

Call each child's name, one by one, referring to the Daily 5 clipboard. On the clipboard, mark their choice in the next blank box using the coding system (R = Read to Self, RS = Read to Someone, W = Work on Writing, WW = Word Work, and L = Listen to Reading). Helpers will keep count for Read to Someone, as we take a maximum of six people for Read to Someone per round. Once kids finish checking in, total how many Read-to-Someone kids there are. It must be even, or someone will have to make a change. Dismiss them in the following order: Listen to Reading first, then Read to Self, followed by Work on Writing, Word Work, and finally the children doing Read to Someone. Since only Read-to-Someone students are left, they will easily be able to find a partner and head out. Dismissing in this manner allows for a calmer start so there is not a mad rush.

At this time I usually pull a small focused reading or writing group and do one-on-one conferences. Today, rather than pull any small groups, please move around the room, reading with kids, helping with their writing, and so on. On my desk, you will find my brown polka-dot conferring notebook. You can use the notebook to guide you as you work with children. Inside is a tabbed section for each child. It will tell you what their goals are in reading and writing, as well as the teaching strategy I have been using to guide their instruction. As you meet with children, their conferring page in the notebook can help you guide your conversation with them. Feel free to jot a note on their conferring page. Your input is valued.

Please spend some time with the students in the Word-Work area. We are working with our youngest learners on letter formation and learning their sight words.

Please make it a priority to spend two to four minutes with the following students during Daily 5: Jesse, Mariah, Micah, and Treven. You will see what we are working on based on their conferring sheets. Read with other students as time permits.

After about twenty to twenty-five minutes, or when kids are showing signs of losing their stamina and focus, ring the chimes (on the square shelves to the left of my desk). Call the kids back up to the green carpet. I usually do a focus lesson here. However, since you are a guest, please have three or four students model for the class their reading strategy this week or share a writing strategy as the focus lesson.

Then, using the clipboard, repeat the above procedure, having students make a choice for round 2. They must make a new choice. Dismiss the group as described above. You'll rotate through the class again, working with different children.

After about twenty to twenty-five minutes, or when their stamina is waning, ring the chimes again to pull them back to the rug, and read through the poems behind the little brown chair by the chart rack. See if the students can locate the new sight words, which are on the whiteboard in the gathering space.

Using the clipboard, have kids check in for round 3, indicating their choice in the next column. They must make a choice that is different from their first two. Dismiss the group as detailed above. Again, you will rotate through the group, working with individuals. Signal with the chimes after about twenty minutes, inviting them back up to the gathering spot.

We end the morning with a share time. Some may want to share writing and some a strategy or a piece of reading.

The children are so well trained that not only can they tell you how to do Daily 5, but they probably *will* tell you how, especially if you veer in any way from their well-internalized routine. If you have any questions, don't hesitate to ask any of the students in the room.

Writing workshop: You will want to preview the lesson before you begin. The lesson should take no more than ten minutes, and then students will proceed to independent writing time. Please use the conferring notebook to guide your conferences with individuals. Come together and allow for a brief time of sharing before preparing for lunch.

11:47 Get ready for lunch.

Even if he or she is completely unfamiliar with the Daily 5, with this plan in hand, the guest teacher should be able to lead students through the familiar routines. And it's true; your children will have no hesitation in setting the guest teacher straight if he or she deviates from their expectations!

New Students to the Class

We all know the feeling of bustling around the room hunting for a student chair for the new student who will be arriving in minutes. Getting a new student at a moment's notice can be a little frustrating and frazzling for a teacher . . . but can you imagine being a new student? Some of you have experienced the anxiety and apprehension that goes with being "the new kid." Others of you were the assigned friend required to lead the guided tour at recess. Whatever our background and experience, we truly want new students to feel welcome and wanted.

For many of us, a regular stream of new students is a normal part of our school culture. Supporting these students by getting them up and running with Daily 5 while honoring the current stamina of the rest of the class doesn't have to upset the apple cart. In fact, they provide opportunities for fine tuning and additional growth. Here are ideas that will support the new student, give existing students a sense of ownership, and help you remain positive and focused on good instruction.

When a new student arrives, take the opportunity to review the Daily 5 I-charts with the whole class (including student modeling). Everyone will benefit from the reminders and explicit review.

Assign a student or pair of students each day to be Daily 5 helpers. Our younger students get to wear a simple vest, which easily identifies them as the day's helper. New students shadow the helper, following along, doing what the helper does, from checking in to staying in one place to gathering and putting away materials. If the partnership is going well and both parties choose, we let them continue for a few days until the new students experience each of the Daily 5 and the different places to sit around the room, and build their stamina. Because new students' stamina may not be as strong as their peers', we often pull them aside when their stamina wanes to do assessments and teach them how to choose good-fit books. We find it important that we not always select the same student to partner with new classmates so the new student gets to know as many children as possible, and vice versa.

What happens when more than one new student arrives on the same day or within a week? We begin a regular whole-class focus lesson. After the existing class members check in and start their first round of Daily 5, we keep new students together in a small group, and during each round of Daily 5 they participate in the 10 Steps to Independence. The new students build their own I-charts, practice behaviors, and build stamina together.

Parents

Just as we are explicit in letting our students in on what they are going to be learning and why, we are excited to include their families because we know that the more they understand what their children are doing during the day at school, the more they will be able to support them at home.

Sometimes the changes we make to the environment or the curriculum can be difficult for parents. Teaching is one of the few professions in which everyone has experience to draw on, because we all went to school. We help our parents transition to a way of doing school that doesn't match their experience by educating them about what we are doing. Parents have a right to know what their children will be learning and how they will be spending their time, and we want to assure them of our vast teaching knowledge and the care we have for their children. Since a structure such as the Daily 5 may look vastly different from their own schooling, a letter at the beginning of the year can help answer questions, dispel fears, and start the open communication we want with our parents.

Here is a sample letter introducing the Daily 5 (also in Appendix H):

Dear Parents and Guardians,

Welcome to a new school year! I hope you had a wonderful summer and enjoyed spending quality time with your child. I know that each year of your child's schooling presents new expectations and routines for you and your child to become familiar with. I will be introducing classroom routines and structure in a way that removes all of the guesswork from the child and allows them to concentrate fully on learning. In reading, the classroom structure I use is called Daily 5. Soon your child will be talking about "the Daily 5" at home. The purpose of this letter is to explain to you what the Daily 5 is and what you should expect to see at home.

The Daily 5 is a literacy structure that teaches independence and gives children the skills needed to create a lifetime love of reading and writing. It consists of five tasks that are introduced individually. When introduced to each task, the children discuss what it looks like, sounds like, and feels like to engage in the task independently. Then, the children work on building their stamina until they are successful at being independent while doing that task.

These are the five tasks:

- *Read to Self*
- *Work on Writing*
- *Read to Someone*
- *Listen to Reading*
- *Word Work*

When all five tasks have been introduced and the children are fully engaged in reading and writing, I am able to work with small groups and confer with children one-on-one. This structure is effective, the results are amazing, and the children look forward to Daily 5 time.

One thing you will notice is a decrease in the number of worksheets your child brings home. Although worksheets keep students busy, they don't result in the high level of learning we want for your child.

Ask your child about Daily 5 and Math Daily 3 and see what they have to say. I anticipate your child will tell you about the class stamina and how we are working toward independence, and maybe you will even hear about some of the fantastic things your child has written, read, or listened to during our Daily 5 time. Please feel free to contact me with any questions you may have.

Thank you for your continued support!

Trusting Our Students and Our Teaching

By now you have the basic tools to get the Daily 5 up and running in your classrooms. Taking the time to launch Daily 5, allowing children to build their stamina slowly, and knowing it won't be perfect right off (it never is for us either!) is paying it forward for a calmer and more productive year. Now it's time to look back at the core beliefs that underpin the Daily 5, particularly trust.

When we first began developing the Daily 5, we constantly reflected, wondering if students were really reading, writing, and learning. We had to allow for some initial discomfort that came from not being able to "see" what they were learning as we had in the past. Gone were the smiling paper sack character puppets, the stacks of activity sheets, the forms and surveys. We truly believed those activities had been inauthentic busywork that did not support student growth, and certainly weren't signs of learning, but their absence created a sense of disequilibrium.

Margaret Mooney once said something that struck a chord with us: "Independence is synonymous with accountability." And she was right. With each step of this journey, we teach our students to build their stamina. We create a sense of urgency for their work. We teach them the desired behaviors. They become independent. Our children help us learn to trust our teaching and prove they deserve to be trusted to be independent. Our students rise to our high expectations, they meet high standards, and they willingly accept the responsibility to do so.

We read research, talk about research, and allow the experts in our field to give us the courage to trust our teaching and trust our students and their need for extensive amounts of practice in reading and writing in order to become proficient. And proficient they become. Over the years of our work in developing and using the Daily 5, many of you have shared the success stories of your children's growth as measured by beginning, middle, and end-of-year assessments. We are extremely proud and humbled by the progress made by all our students as active participants in the Daily 5.

Since the publication of our first Daily 5 book, our learning has continued, and still continues, to grow and change. This book represents the state of our current thinking. It is a privilege that so many of you have joined us on this journey of supporting students to become the best readers and writers they can be through teaching, trusting, providing choice, and honoring each student. Change comes slowly, and it is through your tireless work with children and willingness to treat each student and each class as the remarkable individuals they are that we are all slowly but surely making a huge impact on education.

Stamina Chart

STAMINA									
25									
24									
23									
22									
21									
20									
19									
18									
17									
16									
15									
14									
13									
12									
11									
10									
9									
8									
7									
6									
5									
4									
3									
2									
1									

Minutes

The 10 Steps to Independence for Read to Self

Foundation Lesson

Teach this lesson before launching Read to Self:
- Three Ways to Read a Book
  (Note: We teach just one Read-to-Self foundation lesson before the launch. Other foundation lessons for Read to Self are taught subsequently as focus lessons during the launch of Read to Self. They are listed at the bottom of the page.)

Launch

Use the 10 Steps to Independence to launch Read to Self:
Step 1. Identify what is to be taught: Read to Self.
Step 2. Set a purpose and create a sense of urgency for Read to Self:
- It is the best way to become better readers.
- It is fun.
Step 3. Record desirable behaviors of Read to Self on an I-chart.

Sample I-Chart

Read to Self
Independent

Students	Teacher
Read the whole time Stay in one spot Read quietly Get started right away Work on reading stamina	Works with students

Step 4. Model most-desirable behaviors.
Step 5. Model least-desirable behaviors, then most-desirable behaviors again.
Step 6. Place students around the room.
Step 7. Practice and build stamina.
Step 8. Stay out of the way.
Step 9. Use a quiet signal to bring students back to the gathering place.
Step 10. Conduct a group check-in; ask, "How did it go?"

Foundation Lessons

Teach the following as focus lessons during the launch of Read to Self:
- Three Ways to Read a Book (reteach during launch in addition to before launch)
- Choose a Successful Spot
- I PICK Good-Fit Books

The 10 Steps to Independence for Work on Writing

Foundation Lessons

Teach these lessons before launching Work on Writing:
- Underline Words You Don't Know How to Spell, and Move On
- Set Up a Notebook
- Choose What to Write About

Launch

Use the 10 Steps to Independence to launch Work on Writing.

Step 1. Identify what is to be taught: Work on Writing

Step 2. Set a purpose and create a sense of urgency for Work on Writing:
- It helps us become better writers.
- It helps us become better readers.
- It increases fluency of writing.
- It is fun.

Step 3. Record the desired behaviors of Work on Writing on an I-chart.

Sample I-Chart

Work on Writing
Independent

Students	Teacher
Write the whole time Stay in one spot Work quietly Get started right away Work on writing stamina	Works with students

Step 4. Model most-desirable behaviors.

Step 5. Model least-desirable behaviors, then most desirable behaviors again.

Step 6. Place students around the room.

Step 7. Practice and build stamina.

Step 8. Stay out of the way.

Step 9. Use a quiet signal to bring students back to the gathering place.

Step 10. Conduct a group check-in; ask, "How did it go?"

The 10 Steps to Independence for Read to Someone

Foundation Lessons

Teach these lessons before launching Read to Someone:
- EEKK (elbow, elbow, knee, knee)
- Voice Level
- Check for Understanding
- How Partners Read
- How to Get Started
- Coaching or Time?
- How to Choose a Partner

Launch

Use the 10 Steps to Independence to launch Read to Someone.

Step 1. Identify what is to be taught: Read to Someone

Step 2. Set a purpose and create a sense of urgency for Read to Someone.
- It helps us improve our fluency.
- It helps us practice Check for Understanding and Comprehension.
- It is fun.

Step 3. Record the desirable behaviors of Read to Someone on an I-chart.

Sample I-Chart

Read to Someone
Independent

Students	Teacher
Read the whole time Stay in one spot Read quietly Get started right away Work on reading stamina Check for understanding	Works with students

Step 4. Model most-desirable behaviors.

Step 5. Model least-desirable behaviors, then most-desirable behaviors again.

Step 6. Place students around the room.

Step 7. Practice and build stamina.

Step 8. Stay out of the way.

Step 9. Use a quiet signal to bring students back to the gathering place.

Step 10. Conduct a group check-in; ask, "How did it go?"

The Daily 5, Second Edition: Fostering Literacy Independence in the Elementary Grades by Gail Boushey and Joan Moser ("The 2 Sisters"). Copyright © 2014. Stenhouse Publishers.

The 10 Steps to Independence for Listen to Reading

Foundation Lessons

Teach these lessons before launching Listen to Reading:
- Set Up and Clean Up the Technology
- Listen and Follow Along
- Manage Fairness and Equitable Use with a Limited Number of Devices

Launch

Use the 10 Steps of Independence to launch Listen to Reading:

Step 1. Identify what is to be taught: Listen to Reading.

Step 2. Set a purpose and create a sense of urgency for Listen to Reading.
- It helps us become better readers.
- It helps us learn and understand new words.
- It is fun.

Step 3. Record the desirable behaviors of Listen to Reading on an I-chart.

Sample I-Chart

Listen to Reading
Independent

Students	Teacher
Get materials out	Works with students
Listen the whole time	
May listen to another story if time	
Follow along using pictures and/or words	
Stay in one spot	
Listen quietly	
Get started quickly	
Put materials away neatly	

Step 4. Model most-desirable behaviors.

Step 5. Model least-desirable behaviors, then most-desirable behaviors again.

Step 6. Place students around the room.

Step 7. Practice and build stamina.

Step 8. Stay out of the way.

Step 9. Use a quiet signal to bring students back to the gathering place.

Step 10. Conduct a group check-in; ask, "How did it go?"

Appendix F

The 10 Steps to Independence for Word Work

Foundation Lessons
Teach these lessons before launching Word Work:
- Set Up and Clean Up Materials
- Choose Materials and Words to Use
- Choose a Successful Spot

Launch
Use the 10 Steps to Independence to launch Word Work.
Step 1. Identify what is to be taught: Word Work.
Step 2. Set a purpose and create a sense of urgency for Word Work.
- It helps us become better readers, writers, and spellers.
- It is fun.
Step 3. Record the desirable behaviors of Word Work on an I-chart.
Step 4. Model most-desirable behaviors.
Step 5. Model least-desirable behaviors, then most-desirable behaviors again.
Step 6. Place students around the room.
Step 7. Practice and build stamina.
Step 8. Stay out of the way.
Step 9. Use a quiet signal to bring students back to the gathering place.
Step 10. Conduct a group check-in; ask, "How did it go?"

Optional Materials for Word Work
Individual whiteboards, whiteboard table
Magnet letters
Beans
Letter stamps
Colored markers
Clay

Sample I-Charts

Set Up Materials
Independent

Students	Teacher
Get materials out Choose a location where you and others can be successful Set up quietly Stay in one spot Get started quickly	Works with students

The 10 Steps to Independence for Word Work (continued)

How to Use Materials
Independent

Students	Teacher
Work the whole time Stay in one spot except to get and return materials May return one set of materials and get another set to work with before round is over Work quietly Work on stamina Try your best	Works with students

Clean Up Materials
Independent

Students	Teacher
Everyone using materials helps put them away Materials go back in their original container Return materials to the same spot Leave materials neat Clean quietly Get started cleaning right away Clean quickly	Works with students

Choose a Successful Spot

Using gradual release of responsibility, we start by placing students around the room. Following the same ten steps as all of the other Daily 5 options, the students learn to choose where to sit by using the 10 Steps to Independence for Choosing a Successful Spot.

Sample Guest Teacher Plans

Welcome! Thanks so much for coming! This wonderful group of children responds very well to kind, positive words. They are very independent and know the routines well, so I'm sure your day will run smoothly. Don't hesitate to honor them by following their lead; they are a great group.

Schedule at a Glance

8:40–8:55 Students enter the classroom when they arrive at school (open campus) and begin book shopping.
8:55 School starts: attendance, welcome, etc.
9:00–9:15 Calendar
9:15–11:50 Daily 5 and writing workshop
11:50–12:50 Lunch and recess
12:50–2:00 Math
2:00–2:30 Third block (Flex Block: Science/SS, Handwriting, Art)
2:30–2:50 Recess
2:50–3:20 Chapter book
3:20 Dismissal

Students will begin coming into the room about 8:40 or whenever they arrive at school. Please remind them to (1) order lunch, (2) check in on the Daily Graph, (3) grab their book boxes, (4) read or shop for "good-fit books." They will do this until the bell rings at 8:55.

8:55 Day begins: Ask helpers to count up lunches. You will record lunches and absent students on the attendance report, which is in the blue folder. Helpers will take this report to the office. The daily helpers will assist you throughout the day.

Review the schedule with students. Ask if they can make a true statement about the Daily Graph.

Stand and recite the flag salute, and then have the helpers lead the class over to the math calendar.

9:00 Calendar: The helpers will begin leading the calendar. You act as a participant as the helpers manage and run the calendar time.

Move into shared reading on the carpet: Today's literature selection is _____. We are working on modeling fluency as well as the strategy Back Up and Reread as a way to fix up Check for Understanding if and when comprehension breaks down or when a word is read incorrectly.

Daily 5

Here is the structure of Daily 5:

Call each child's name, one by one, referring to the Daily 5 clipboard. On the clipboard, mark their choice in the next blank box using the coding system (R = Read to Self, RS = Read to Someone, W = Work on Writing, WW = Word Work, and L = Listen to Reading). Helpers will keep count for Read to Someone, as we take a maximum of six people for Read to Someone per round. Once kids finish checking in, total how many Read-to-Someone kids there are. It must be even, or someone will have to make a change. Dismiss them in the following order:

Sample Guest Teacher Plans (continued)

Listen to Reading first, then Read to Self, followed by Work on Writing, Word Work, and finally the children doing Read to Someone. Since only Read to Someone students are left, they will easily be able to find a partner and head out. Dismissing in this manner allows for a calmer start so there is not a mad rush.

At this time I usually pull a small focused reading or writing group and do one-on-one conferences. Today, rather than pull any small groups, please move around the room, reading with kids, helping with their writing, and so on. On my desk, you will find my brown polka-dot conferring notebook. You can use the notebook to guide you as you work with children. Inside is a tabbed section for each child. It will tell you what their goals are in reading and writing, as well as the teaching strategy I have been using to guide their instruction. As you meet with children, their conferring page in the notebook can help you guide your conversation with them. Feel free to jot a note on their conferring page. Your input is valued.

Please spend some time with the students in the Word-Work area. We are working with our youngest learners on letter formation and learning their sight words.

Please make it a priority to spend two to four minutes with the following students during Daily 5: Jesse, Mariah, Micah, and Treven. You will see what we are working on based on their conferring sheets. Read with other students as time permits.

After about twenty to twenty-five minutes, or when kids are showing signs of losing their stamina and focus, ring the chimes (on the square shelves to the left of my desk). Call the kids back up to the green carpet. I usually do a focus lesson here. However, since you are a guest, please have three or four students model for the class their reading strategy this week or share a writing strategy as the focus lesson.

Then, using the clipboard, repeat the above procedure, having students make a choice for round 2. They must make a new choice. Dismiss the group as described above. You'll rotate through the class again, working with different children.

After about twenty to twenty-five minutes, or when their stamina is waning, ring the chimes again to pull them back to the rug, and read through the poems behind the little brown chair by the chart rack. See if the students can locate the new sight words, which are on the whiteboard in the gathering space.

Using the clipboard, have kids check in for round 3, indicating their choice in the next column. They must make a choice that is different from their first two. Dismiss the group as detailed above. Again, you will rotate through the group, working with individuals. Signal with the chimes after about twenty minutes, inviting them back up to the gathering spot.

We end the morning with a share time. Some may want to share writing and some a strategy or a piece of reading.

The children are so well trained that not only can they tell you how to do Daily 5, but they probably will tell you how, especially if you veer in any way from their well-internalized routine. If you have any questions, don't hesitate to ask any of the students in the room.

Writing workshop: You will want to preview the lesson before you begin. The lesson should take no more than ten minutes, and then students will proceed to independent writing time. Please use the conferring notebook to guide your conferences with individuals. Come together and allow for a brief time of sharing before preparing for lunch.

11:47 Get ready for lunch.

Sample Parent Letter

Dear Parents and Guardians,

Welcome to a new school year! I hope you had a wonderful summer and enjoyed spending quality time with your child. I know that each year of your child's schooling presents new expectations and routines for you and your child to become familiar with. I will be introducing classroom routines and structure in a way that removes all of the guesswork from the child and allows them to concentrate fully on learning. In reading, the classroom structure I use is called Daily 5. Soon your child will be talking about "the Daily 5" at home. The purpose of this letter is to explain to you what the Daily 5 is and what you should expect to see at home.

The Daily 5 is a literacy structure that teaches independence and gives children the skills needed to create a lifetime love of reading and writing. It consists of five tasks that are introduced individually. When introduced to each task, the children discuss what it looks like, sounds like, and feels like to engage in the task independently. Then, the children work on building their stamina until they are successful at being independent while doing that task.

These are the five tasks:

- Read to Self
- Work on Writing
- Read to Someone
- Listen to Reading
- Word Work

When all five tasks have been introduced and the children are fully engaged in reading and writing, I am able to work with small groups and confer with children one-on-one. This structure is effective, the results are amazing, and the children look forward to Daily 5 time.

One thing you may notice is a decrease in the number of worksheets your child brings home. Although worksheets keep students busy, they don't result in the high level of learning we want for your child.

Ask your child about Daily 5 and Math Daily 3 and see what they have to say. I anticipate your child will tell you about the class stamina and how we are working toward independence, and maybe you will even hear about some of the fantastic things your child has written, read, or listened to during our Daily 5 time. Please feel free to contact me with any questions you may have.

Thank you for your continued support!

Lesson Plans for Launching the Daily 5 and CAFE

Visual color cues for lesson structure:

Foundation Lesson

Brain Break

Focus Lesson: Reading Skill/Strategy

Focus Lesson: Your Specific Reading Skill/Strategy

Sharing

Review

*(All times are approximate. Adjust as needed,
and what doesn't fit today, move to tomorrow.)*

Day 1

8:45 Foundation Lesson. **Read to Self: Three Ways to Read a Book** (see page 68)
Teach the first two ways to read a book, read the pictures and read the words; save
retell a story for another lesson. Introduce the quiet signal for getting students' attention. We use chimes. Let children know its purpose and what it sounds like.

8:53 Brain Break. (approx. 3 min.) Ask children to stand and walk to someone and
tell that classmate one way to read a book. Students will return to their place in the
gathering area after they finish or when they hear the quiet signal.

8:55 Introduce Read to Self; use 10 Steps to Independence (see page 71)
1. "Today we are going to learn to Read to Self. *(Create I-chart and explain
   that the I is for independence.)*
2. "We learn to Read to Self because it is the best way to become a reader and
   it is fun!" *(Write these on the top of the I-chart.)*
3. Record two behaviors on the I-chart that are the most crucial to student
   success.
   • Read the whole time
   • Stay in one spot
   • Get started right away
   • Work quietly
   • Build stamina
4. Have Jaxon model the most desirable behaviors. As he models, review the I-
   chart and ask, "Will Jaxon become a better reader if he does these things?"
5. Have Olivia model least-desirable behaviors. Review the I-chart and ask,
   "Will Olivia be a better reader if she does these things?" and then ask her to
   model the most-desirable behaviors. Review the I-chart again and ask the
   same question: "Will Olivia become a better reader if she does these things?"
6. Place students around the room.

Lesson Plans for Launching the Daily 5 and CAFE (continued)

7. Practice and build stamina; see if they can make it three minutes, but stop as soon as stamina is gone.
8. Stay out of the way.
9. Signal when stamina is broken; return to the gathering area.
10. Conduct a group check-in and fill in the stamina chart (see page 46)

9:20 Foundation Lesson. **Read to Self: I PICK Good-Fit Books** (see page 73)

9:30 Review **Read-to-Self I-chart and practice again.**
- This time either try again for three minutes if they didn't make it the first time, or try for four minutes. We would love students to build stamina quickly, but the ultimate goal is to build by one minute each practice time. If we build too quickly, it may not be sustainable.
- Be sure to stay out of the way and call students back as soon as stamina is gone.
- Group check-in: How did it go? Fill in stamina chart (see page 46).

9:45 Foundation Lesson. **Read to Someone: Check for Understanding** (see page 93)

9:55 Brain Break. (Song)

10:00 Focus Lesson: Reading Skill/Strategy Lesson. Getting to know the CAFE board/Review Check for Understanding. Choose a child to write the strategy on a card and post the card on the CAFE board.

10:10 Foundation Lesson. **Read to Self: Review the first two ways to read a book and add the third way to read a book.** Model retelling the story from earlier. Teacher retells pages 1 and 2. Call on students to retell the remaining pages. Add "Retell a story" to the I-chart for Three Ways to Read a Book.

10:20 Brain Break. Ask students to turn and talk to elbow buddy and discuss the three ways to read a book.

10:25 Review what we did today and what we will do tomorrow. "Today you had _____ minutes of stamina when you were doing Read to Self. Tomorrow we are going to try for _____ minutes of stamina. Do you think we can do it? I do too! I am so excited, because you are going to be such good readers!"

Teacher reflective notes: Day 1 was very successful. The first practice of stamina building I had one student who tried to talk to a student around him. Everyone else was on task, but I knew I couldn't let it go so I used the signal to call students back. When they came back, we reviewed the I-chart and emphasized "Read the whole time" and "Stay in one spot." We filled in the stamina chart to a little under one minute to reflect how long they made it. I also asked children if they knew what a "bubble space" was. I explained that when you find a place to sit to work, you pre-

Lesson Plans for Launching the Daily 5 and CAFE (continued)

tend a bubble is all around you, and this is your "bubble space." You do not want to pop someone's bubble by getting too close. The second round of stamina building was much more successful, and students made it three minutes. Tomorrow I will use Jeffery to help me model behaviors.

Day 2

8:45 Review **Read-to-Self I-chart and build stamina.**
- Review the chart and have a student model it the right way (either Hadley or Griffin). Ask, "Will _____ become a better reader if he [or she] does these things?"
- Have Jeffery model it the wrong way and then the right way. Ask, "Will Jeffery become a better reader if he does these things?"
- Build stamina. Try for four minutes. Be sure to stay out of the way.
- Group check-in: How did it go? Fill in stamina chart (see page 46).

9:05 Foundation Lesson. **Read to Self: Review Three Ways to Read a Book** (page 68) **I PICK Good-Fit Books** (page 73)

9:15 Build Read-to-Self stamina again.
- Try for five minutes, or one minute more than last practice time.
- Group check-in: How did it go? Fill in stamina chart (see page 46).

9:25 Foundation Lesson. **Work on Writing: Underline Words . . .** (see page 81)

9:35 Brain Break. (Song)

9:40 Foundation Lesson. **Work on Writing: Set Up a Notebook** (see page 89)

9:50 Brain Break. (Poem)

9:55 Foundation Lesson. **Word Work: Set Up Materials** (see page 102)

10:05 Brain Break. (Story)

10:10 Foundation Lesson. **Read to Someone: EEKK** (see page 92) (As a reminder, students practice these foundation lessons as we teach them, but they aren't actually doing the task of Read to Someone until all of the foundation lessons have been taught and practiced.)

10:20 Brain Break. (Hand jive)

10:25 Review what we did today and what we will do tomorrow. "Today you had _____ minutes of stamina when you were Reading to Self. Tomorrow we are going to try for _____ minutes of stamina. Do you think we can do it? I do too! I am so proud of all of your hard work!"

Lesson Plans for Launching the Daily 5 and CAFE (continued)

Teacher reflective notes: Today the class would have made it four minutes the first try, but Jeffery struggled again and I had to call everyone back. We revisited the I-chart, and the second time we tried for four minutes and they made it. I am hopeful the class will be able to build up to six minutes tomorrow. I noticed that the brain breaks work better when I incorporate movement. I am going to put my poem chart in the back of the room, and we will move there when we read our poems. Our class goes to the library in a few days, so I want to do another lesson on good-fit books and a lesson or two on I PICK so they can use that information when choosing books. Then, I may have a few students model their book choice for the class.

Day 3

8:45 Foundation Lesson. **Read to Self: Three Ways to Read a Book and I PICK Good-Fit Books**

8:55 Review **Read-to-Self I-chart and build stamina.**
- Review the I-chart and have a student model it the right way. (Adilyn)
- Have Trenton model behaviors the wrong way and then the right way.
- Build stamina: Try for five minutes, or one minute more than last time. Be sure to stay out of the way.
- Group check-in: How did it go? Fill in stamina chart (see page 46).

9:15 Foundation Lesson. **Read to Self: I-PICK Good-Fit Books** (page 73)

9:25 Build Read-to-Self stamina again.
- Try for one minute longer than yesterday.
- Group check-in: How did it go? Fill in stamina chart (page 46).

9:35 Foundation Lesson. **Work on Writing: Underline Words . . .** (see page 81)

9:45 Brain Break. (Song)

9:50 Foundation Lesson. **Read to Someone: Review EEKK/I Read, You Read** (see page 92)

10:00 Brain Break. (Poem)

10:05 Foundation Lesson. **Word Work: Set Up and Clean Up Materials** (see page 102)

10:15 Brain Break. (Song)

10:20 Focus Lesson: Reading Skill/Strategy. Back Up and Reread (refer to "Ready Reference Guide" in *The CAFE Book*, Boushey and Moser 2009)

10:25 Review what we did today and what we will do tomorrow. "Today you had _____ minutes of stamina when you were Reading to Self. Tomorrow we are going

Lesson Plans for Launching the Daily 5 and CAFE (continued)

to try for _____ minutes of stamina. Do you think we can do it? I do too! We are going to be such good readers!"

Teacher reflective notes: We did it today! The whole class made it five minutes the first time and six minutes the second time. I have followed the 10 Steps explicitly, so I let Jeffery come in for a few minutes at recess to practice. We reviewed the I-chart and he was successful practicing for three minutes before I sent him outside. I am hopeful this will help for tomorrow. If not, I will let him stay in again for a few minutes at recess time. I was running short on time so I had to cut the CAFE strategy lesson short. I will revisit it tomorrow and have a student create the strategy card. I also want to be sure to do another lesson on I-PICK tomorrow to prepare them for library. The goal tomorrow is to try for eight minutes and nine minutes.

Day 4

8:45 Foundation Lesson. **Read to Self: I PICK Good-Fit Books** (see page 73). Pass out bookmarks found on website. Encourage students to use what they learned when looking for books at library today.

8:55 Review **Read-to-Self I-chart and build stamina.**
- Review the I-chart. Discuss how to choose your own place to read (bubble space).
- Let children choose their reading space. Build stamina. Try for one minute longer than yesterday. Be sure to stay out of the way.
- Group check-in: How did it go? Fill in stamina chart (see page 46).

9:10 Foundation Lesson. **Work on Writing: Underline Words . . ./What to Write About** (see page 81)

9:20 Build Read-to-Self stamina.
- Try for one minute longer than earlier today.
- Group check-in: How did it go? Fill in stamina chart (see page 46).

9:35 Foundation Lesson. **Read to Someone: I Read, You Read** (see page 95)

9:45 Brain Break. (Song)

9:50 Foundation Lesson. **Read to Self: How to Book Shop** (see page 73)
- Review our in-class expectations.

10:00 Brain Break. (Poem)

10:05 Foundation Lesson. **Word Work: Review Set Up and Clean Up Materials** (see page 102)
- Teach "choosing materials and words to use"

Lesson Plans for Launching the Daily 5 and CAFE (continued)

10:15 Brain Break. (Song)

10:20 Focus Lesson: Reading Skill/Strategy. Back Up and Reread (refer to "Ready Reference Guide" from *The CAFE Book*)
- Review, have a student create a strategy card, and add the card to the CAFE board.

10:30 Review what we did today and what we will do tomorrow. "Today you had _____ minutes of stamina when you were doing Read to Self. You also were able to choose where you sat! Tomorrow we are going to try for _____ minutes of stamina. *And* we are going to introduce the next Daily 5, Work on Writing!"

Teacher reflective notes: Stamina building was successful today! Jeffery did a good job and was so proud of himself when he was done. I am glad I taught the good-fit book lesson and I PICK before library as it really helped my students. My lesson on book shopping went a little long, but with this group of students I knew it was necessary. Tomorrow I will introduce Work on Writing.

Day 5

8:45 Foundation Lesson. **Read to Self: Review I PICK Good-Fit Books/Three Ways to Read a Book**

8:55 Review **Read-to-Self I-chart and build stamina.**
- Review the chart.
- Build stamina. Try for ten minutes, or one minute more than yesterday. This time, meet with students to assess and to set goals.
- Group check-in: How did it go? Fill in stamina chart (see page 46).

9:10 Introduce Work on Writing using 10 Steps to Independence.
1. "Today we are going to learn to do Work on Writing." *(Create I-chart and explain that I is for independent.)*
2. "We learn to do Work on Writing because it helps us become better readers and writers, and it is *fun*!" *(Write these on the top of the I-chart.)*
3. Record on the I-chart the five behaviors that are most crucial to student success.
   - Work the whole time
   - Stay in one spot
   - Get started right away
   - Work quietly
   - Build stamina
4. Ask Camden to model the most-desirable behaviors. As he's modeling, review the I-chart and ask, "Will Camden become a better writer if he does these things?"

Lesson Plans for Launching the Daily 5 and CAFE (continued)

5. Ask Janya to model least-desirable behaviors. As she's modeling, review the I-chart and ask, "Will Janya be a better writer if she does these things?" and then ask her to model the most-desirable behaviors. Review the I-chart again and ask the same question, "Will Janya be a better writer if she does these things?"
6. Place students around the room.
7. Practice and build stamina.
8. Stay out of the way.
9. Signal when stamina is broken.
10. Group check-in: How did it go? Fill in stamina chart (see page 46).

9:25 Foundation Lesson. **Work on Writing: What to Write About** (see page 90)

9:35 Review **Work-on-Writing I-chart and practice again.**
- This time either students try again for the same number of minutes of stamina as the last try or I'll encourage them to try for one more minute.
- Be sure to stay out of the way and call students back as soon as stamina is broken.
- Group check-in: How did it go? Fill in stamina chart (see page 46).

9:50 Foundation Lesson. **Read to Someone: Review EEKK and I Read, You Read** (see page 95)

10:00 Brain break. (Song)

10:05 Focus Lesson: Reading Skill/Strategy. **Review Check for Understanding** (see page 93)

10:15 Brain Break. (Poem)

10:20 Sharing. Allow a few students a chance to share what they did during Daily 5.

10:25 Review what we did today and what we will do tomorrow. "Today we had _____ minutes of stamina when you were doing Read to Self, and we learned how to do Work on Writing. We even made it _____ minutes in Work on Writing! Way to go!"

Teacher reflective notes: My students actually groaned when I called them back at the end of their first Work-on-Writing time. Janya struggles with writing, so I need to make a point to meet with her to discuss writing options. Our list of what to write about is full of great ideas. Eventually I am going to introduce the writing calendars from the www.thedailycafe.com so students will have that option as well. I ran short on time for sharing because my strategy lesson went a little long. I need to be sure to not cut out sharing, because it is so important to student success.

Lesson Plans for Launching the Daily 5 and CAFE (continued)

Day 6

8:45 Focus Lesson: Reading Skill/Strategy Lesson. Use Prior Knowledge to Connect with Text (use "Ready Reference Guide" from *The CAFE Book*)

8:55 Read to Self: Stamina building—twelve minutes? The goal is truly one minute longer than yesterday; it is all about the class you have in front of you.
- While students are building reading stamina, individually meet with students to assess and set goals.
- When stamina wanes, sound signal and return to gathering area.
- Group check-in: How did it go? Fill in stamina chart (see page 46).

9:10 Foundation Lesson. Core Belief: Review Chimes and Transitions as Brain and Body Breaks (see page 32)
- Create an I-chart about what transition time should look like and sound like when students move to and from their self-selected Daily 5 work space.

9:20 Review Work-on-Writing I-chart and build stamina.
- Review the chart and have a student model the behaviors the right way (Natalie). Then ask, "Will Natalie become a better writer if she does these things?"
- Have Seth model the behaviors the wrong way and then the right way, and ask the question after each attempt, "Will Seth become a better writer if he does these things?"
- Build stamina. Try for one minute longer than they were able to write yesterday. Be sure to stay out of the way.
- Group check-in: How did it go? Fill in stamina chart (see page 46).

9:35 Focus Lesson: Reading Skill/Strategy
- Combine Check for Understanding and Back Up and Reread (use "Ready Reference Guide" from *The CAFE Book*).

9:45 Build writing stamina again
- Try for one minute longer than earlier today.
- Group check-in: How did it go? Fill in stamina chart (see page 46).

9:55 Foundation Lesson. Listen to Reading: Set Up the Technology (see page 101)
- Introduce the devices for Listen to Reading and, using a projector, show how to access Listen-to-Reading websites and what to do.

10:05 Brain Break. (Song)

10:10 Focus Lesson: Your Specific Reading Skill/Strategy. This is a time we teach strategies that are specific to our class or grade level or that are required by our district or board. We teach the strategies from the CAFE Menu and use the corresponding resources for those strategies. Here, you may need to use your own specific resource; this is where it would be used.

Lesson Plans for Launching the Daily 5 and CAFE (continued)

10:22 Sharing. Allow a few students a chance to share what they did during Daily 5.

10:30 Review what we did today and what we will do tomorrow.

Teacher reflective notes: Today's foundation lesson prepared students for when they go to the computer lab tomorrow and will get to access the site on their own. I will preteach a few of the optional sites for Listen to Reading before Listen to Reading is launched in the classroom. Jeffery struggled again today, so I will make a point to conference with him tomorrow during Read to Self, and we will set a behavior goal. Students struggle with opening their Work-on-Writing notebook to the right page, so I will model tomorrow how to mark their page and access it more easily.

Day 7

8:45 Focus Lesson: Your Specific Reading Skill/Strategy. Use prior knowledge to connect with text (use "Ready Reference Guide" from *The CAFE Book*). Ask one student to create the strategy card and then post it for the class on the CAFE board.

8:55 Read to Self stamina building: one minute longer than yesterday
- While students are building reading stamina, individually meet with students to assess and to set goals.
- When stamina falters, sound signal and return to gathering area.
- Group check-in: How did it go? Fill in stamina chart (see page 46).

9:10 Foundation Lesson. **Work on Writing:** Finding and marking your place in the notebook. Teach students to add the date at the top of their writing. Review how to select a topic and get started right away.

9:20 Review **Work-on-Writing I-chart and build stamina.**
- Review the I-chart and have a student model it the right way.
- If students need to see this again, ask one student to model it the wrong way and then the right way again. You may want to drop the incorrect model.
- Build stamina. Set goal of writing for one minute longer than before; be sure to stay out of the way.
- Group check-in: How did it go? Fill in stamina chart (see page 46).

9:35 Focus Lesson: Reading Skill/Strategy. Tune In to Interesting Words (use "Ready Reference Guide" from *The CAFE Book*).

9:45 Build writing stamina again.
- Try for nine minutes, or one minute longer than yesterday.
- Group check-in: How did it go? Fill in stamina chart (see page 46).

Lesson Plans for Launching the Daily 5 and CAFE (continued)

9:55 Focus Lesson: Your Specific Reading Skill/Strategy. This is a time we teach strategies that are specific to our class or grade level or that are required by our district or board. We teach the strategies from the CAFE Menu and use the corresponding resources for those strategies. Here, you may need to use your own specific resource; this is where it would be used.

10:05 Brain Break. (Song)

10:10 Focus Lesson: Reading Skill/Strategy. Review Check for Understanding and I Read, You Read. Use the plastic check mark and demonstrate what Check for Understanding looks like when you do Read with Someone. Call on students to demonstrate and take turns as I model Check for Understanding.

10:22 Sharing. Allow a few students a chance to share what they did during Daily 5.

10:30 Review what we did today and what we will do tomorrow.

Teacher reflective notes: Showing students where to start in their notebook was a huge help. I conferred with Jeffery, and while we are building his stamina, I am going to check in with him between conferences. I will taper this off as I see him become more and more successful. After adding the vocabulary strategy on the CAFE board tomorrow, I am going to try to play "Guess My Strategy" so it becomes clearer how these strategies can be used together.

Day 8

8:45 Focus Lesson: Reading Skill/Strategy. Tune In to Interesting Words (use "Ready Reference Guide" from *The CAFE Book*). Ask one student to create the strategy card and then post it for the class on the CAFE board.

8:55 Read to Self: Stamina building
- While students are building reading stamina, individually meet with students to assess and to set goals.
- When stamina falters, sound signal and return to gathering area.
- Group check-in: How did it go? Fill in stamina chart (see page 46).

9:15 Focus Lesson: Reading Skill/Strategy. Play "Guess My Strategy."

9:25 Review Work-on-Writing I-chart and build stamina.
- Review the I-chart.
- Build stamina. Try for one minute longer than yesterday.
- Meet individually with students to assess and to set goals.
- Group check-in: How did it go? Fill in stamina chart (see page 46).

Lesson Plans for Launching the Daily 5 and CAFE (continued)

9:40 Foundation Lesson. **Read to Someone:** How to Choose a Partner (be sure to discuss tone of voice) (see page 98)

9:50 Brain Break. (Story)

9:55 Foundation Lesson. **Read to Someone:** Coaching or Time? (see page 96)

10:05 Brain Break. (Song)

10:10 Focus Lesson: Your Specific Reading Skill/Strategy. This is a time we teach strategies that are specific to our class or grade level or that are required by our district or board. We teach the strategies from the CAFE Menu and use the corresponding resources for those strategies. Here, you may need to use your own specific resource; this is where it would be used.

10:15 Brain Break. (Poem)

10:20 Sharing. Allow a few students a chance to share what they did during Daily 5.

10:25 Review what we did today and what we will do tomorrow.

Teacher reflective notes: Jeffery had a good day today! I checked in with him three times during Read to Self and during Work on Writing, but he was successful. Tomorrow I will do the same and see if he is able to maintain his success. Students loved playing "Guess My Strategy," and I will definitely use this again.

Day 9

INTRODUCE CHOICE!

8:45 Focus Lesson: Reading Skill/Strategy. Read appropriate-level texts that are a good fit (use "Ready Reference Guide" from *The CAFE Book*).

8:55 Round 1 of Daily 5—Introduce Choice! *"Class, I am so excited about our day today. You have learned how to be independent when you do Read to Self and Work on Writing. Today you will be completely in charge of the order in which you do them. Some of you may choose Read to Self first; others may choose Work on Writing. You all know why you are doing each choice and how to be working independently. I trust you to be independent during the time you work on your Daily 5 choice just like you have learned and practiced."*

- Have students close their eyes, picture themselves either reading or writing, and think about which they would rather do first.
- Tell students to be ready. When I call their name they will either say "Read to Self" or "Work on Writing." As they call their choice, mark it on the check-in sheet (see page 112).

Lesson Plans for Launching the Daily 5 and CAFE (continued)

- By this time many classes are up to fifteen minutes of independent work. During this time, meet individually with students to assess and to set goals.
- When stamina runs out, sound signal and return to gathering area.
- Group check-in: How did it go? Fill in stamina chart (see page 46).

9:20 Foundation Lesson. **Read to Someone:** Review Coaching or Time?

9:30 Round 2 of Daily 5
- Review how exciting it was that students were able to choose for their first round of Daily 5. Remind them the two choices at this point are Read to Self and Work on Writing.
- "You are all going to check in again. Be ready; when I call your name you are either going to say Read to Self or Work on Writing, whichever you didn't pick the first time."
- Call on students and use the check-in sheet to record their choices. If they choose the same thing twice, gently remind them to make the other choice.
- Build stamina. Encourage students to work for one minute longer than last round.
- Meet individually with students to assess and to set goals.
- When stamina runs out, sound signal and return to gathering area.
- Group check-in: How did it go? Fill in stamina chart (see page 46).

9:50 Foundation Lesson. **Read to Someone:** Review (from yesterday) How to Choose a Partner and include reminder about voice level and tone (see page 98).

10:00 Brain Break. (Story)

10:05 Focus Lesson: Your Specific Reading Skill/Strategy. This is a time we teach strategies that are specific to our class or grade level or that are required by our district or board. We teach the strategies from the CAFE Menu and use the corresponding resources for those strategies. Here, you may need to use your own specific resource; this is where it would be used.

10:15 Brain Break. (Poem)

10:20 Sharing. Allow a few students a chance to share what they did during Daily 5.

10:25 Review what we did today and what we will do tomorrow.

Teacher reflective notes: Wow! The children were so excited to be able to choose! It was so fun! It took a little longer than I expected for them to check in, but that will go faster with time, I am sure. Due to check-in taking a little longer today, I cut out the poem brain break to be sure to have time for sharing. Jeffery did a good job with his stamina. I did check in with him frequently like yesterday. Tomorrow I am going to continue to check in, but not as frequently and see if that helps.

Lesson Plans for Launching the Daily 5 and CAFE (continued)

Day 10

8:45 Focus Lesson: Reading Skill/Strategy. Read appropriate-level texts that are a good fit (use "Ready Reference Guide" from *The CAFE Book*). This ties in with lessons on good-fit books. Ask one student to create the strategy card and then post it for the class on the CAFE board.

8:55 Round 1 of Daily 5
- Have students close their eyes, picture themselves either reading or writing, and think about which they would rather do first.
- Tell students to be ready. When you call their name they will check in with either Read to Self or Work on Writing. As they call their choice, use the check-in sheet and record it.
- Students build stamina, with a goal of working for one minute longer than yesterday.
- Meet individually with students to assess and to set goals.
- When stamina runs out, sound signal and return to gathering area.
- Group check-in: How did it go? Fill in stamina chart (see page 46).

9:20 Focus Lesson: Reading Skill/Strategy. Check for Understanding/Back Up and Reread (what this looks like when partner reading).

9:30 Round 2 of Daily 5
- Tell students, "Be ready. When I call your name you are going to say either Read to Self or Work on Writing, whichever you didn't pick the first time."
- Call students' names and use the check-in sheet to record their choices. If they choose the same thing twice, gently remind them to make a different choice.
- Build stamina. Try for one more minute than last practice time.
- Meet individually with students to assess and to set goals.
- Group check-in: How did it go? Fill in stamina chart (see page 46).

9:50 Focus Lesson: Reading Skill/Strategy. Tune In to Interesting Words

10:00 Brain Break. (Story)

10:05 Focus Lesson: Your Specific Reading Skill/Strategy. This is a time we teach strategies that are specific to our class or grade level or that are required by our district or board. We teach the strategies from the CAFE Menu and use the corresponding resources for those strategies. Here, you may need to use your own specific resource; this is where it would be used.

10:15 Brain Break. (Poem)

10:20 Sharing. Allow a few students a chance to share what they did during Daily 5.

10:25 Review what we did today and what we will do tomorrow.

Lesson Plans for Launching the Daily 5 and CAFE (continued)

Teacher reflective notes: Today I got a new student. We reviewed the Read-to-Self and Work-on-Writing I-charts, and I paired her with Natalie. I met with her once in the middle of each round to check in and review expectations. She did a nice job and seemed to understand. Tomorrow I will pair her with Drew. The foundation lessons for Read to Someone have been successful, and I am scheduled to introduce Read to Someone tomorrow but I am nervous! Will it work? I hope so! Jeffery was challenged today with staying in one spot, so I met with him and introduced the use of tools. He chose to sit on the floor next to the cupboard. He chose an I Spy book and a fidget for his tools and I gave him a stopwatch and graph paper and began to teach him to graph his reading time and brain break time. I will review this tomorrow with him.

Day 11

8:45 Focus Lesson: Reading Skill/Strategy. Review Check for Understanding and model how it is used with Read to Someone.

8:55 Round 1 of Daily 5
- Have students close their eyes, picture themselves either reading or writing, and think about which they would rather do first.
- Tell students to be ready. When you call their name they will say either "Read to Self" or "Work on Writing." As they call their choice, use the check-in sheet and record it.
- Meet individually with students to assess and to set goals.
- When stamina runs out, sound signal and return to gathering area.
- Group check-in: How did it go? Fill in stamina chart (see page 46).

9:20 Focus Lesson: Your Specific Reading Skill/Strategy; Brain Break. At this time you may consider your strategy lesson as part of the brain break. If the lesson is active, it may act as a brain break and lesson all in one. For example, if students are actively turning and talking during a lesson, that could be the brain break they need while learning something new. At other times, if the lesson is not active, the children may need a stretch or a turn-and-talk activity to rejuvenate their brains. Watch your students; you will know.

9:30 Round 2 of Daily 5
- Tell students, "Be ready; when I call your name you are going to say either Read to Self or Work on Writing, whichever you didn't pick the first time."
- Call on students and use the check-in sheet to record their choices. If they choose the same thing twice, gently remind them.
- Build stamina. Try for twenty minutes. Meet with students to assess and to set goals.
- Group check-in: How did it go? Fill in stamina chart (see page 46).

Lesson Plans for Launching the Daily 5 and CAFE (continued)

9:55 Introduce Read to Someone using the 10 Steps to Independence.

1. "Today we are going to learn to do Read to Someone. *(Create an I-chart and explain that the I is for independent.)*
2. "We learn to do Read to Someone because it helps us become a better reader by improving our fluency and understanding, and it is *fun*!" *(Write these on the top of the I-chart.)*
3. Record on the I-chart the five behaviors that are the most crucial to student success.
    - Read the whole time
    - Stay in one spot
    - Get started right away
    - Read quietly
    - Build reading stamina
4. Have Owen and Mario model the most-desirable behaviors. As they do, review the I-chart and ask, "Will Owen and Mario become better readers if they do these things?"
5. Have Sierra and Sevda model least-desirable behaviors. Review the I-chart and ask, "Will Sierra and Sevda become better readers if they do these things?" Then have the same students model the most-desirable behaviors. Review the I-chart again and ask the same question. "Will Sierra and Sevda become better readers if they do these things?"
6. Place students around the room.
7. Practice and build stamina.
8. Stay out of the way.
9. Signal to gather students when stamina runs out.
10. Group check-in: How did it go? Fill in stamina chart (see page 46).

10:10 Review Read-to-Someone I-chart and practice again.

- This time, either students try again for the same number of minutes of stamina as the last try, or you can encourage them to try for one more minute.
- Be sure to stay out of the way and call students back as soon as stamina runs out.
- Group check-in: How did it go? Fill in stamina chart (see page 46).

10:20 Sharing. Allow a few students a chance to share what they did during Daily 5.

10:25 Review what we did today and what we will do tomorrow.

Teacher reflective notes: Read to Someone was a hit. They love the interaction. It got a little noisy, so I reviewed that during our focus lesson. I also needed to set a higher expectation for sitting close to each other with EEKK. I didn't have enough time to

Lesson Plans for Launching the Daily 5 and CAFE (continued)

review I Read, You Read. I think I will quit graphing stamina for the Read to Self and Work on Writing rounds, because they are solidly improving, but I will keep it for Read to Someone. Jeffery was able to chart his stamina for Reading to Self, which was five minutes, and then his tool time, which was six minutes. I am glad he was honest with himself. We talked about how his goal is to read for more minutes than tool time lasts. We will touch base again tomorrow.

Day 12

8:45 Focus Lesson: Your Specific Reading Skill/Strategy; Brain Break. At this time you may consider your strategy lesson as part of the brain break. If the lesson is active, it may act as a brain break and lesson all in one. For example, if students are actively turning and talking during a lesson, that could be the brain break they need while learning something new. At other times, if the lesson is not active, the children may need a stretch or a turn-and-talk activity to rejuvenate their brains. Watch your students; you will know.

8:55 Round 1 of Daily 5
- Tell students to be ready. When you call their name they will say either "Read to Self" or "Work on Writing." As they call their choice, use the check-in sheet and record it.
- Students build stamina, with a goal of working for one minute longer than yesterday.
- Meet individually with students to assess and to set goals.
- When stamina runs out, sound signal and return to gathering area.
- Group check-in: How did it go? Fill in stamina chart (see page 46).

9:20 Focus Lesson: Your Specific Reading Skill/Strategy; Brain Break

9:30 Round 2 of Daily 5
- Tell students, "Be ready; when I call your name you are going to say either Read to Self or Work on Writing, whichever you didn't pick the first time."
- Call on students and use the check-in sheet to record their choices. If they choose the same thing twice, gently remind them to make a different choice.
- Students build stamina, with a goal of working for one minute longer than yesterday.
- Meet individually with students to assess and to set goals.
- When stamina runs out, sound signal and return to gathering area.
- Group check-in: How did it go? Fill in stamina chart (see page 46).

9:55 Review Read-to-Someone I-chart and practice again.
- Place students with partners around the room. Encourage them to try to build their stamina by one minute from yesterday.

Lesson Plans for Launching the Daily 5 and CAFE (continued)

- Be sure to stay out of the way and call students back as soon as stamina is broken.
- Group check-in: How did it go? Fill in stamina chart (see page 46).

10:20 Sharing. Allow a few students a chance to share what they did during Daily 5.

10:25 Review what we did today and what we will do tomorrow.

Teacher reflective notes: The class is building stamina with reading and also with our focus lessons. It felt right today to incorporate movement with the focus lesson so the brain and body break could be connected to the teaching of the lesson. I know there will be times when I will need to do a movement like a hand jive or stand and touch your toes, which has nothing to do with the lesson, but most of the time I will be able to incorporate a turn and talk, or stand, turn, and talk. It feels like we are truly flying at this point; we were able to add Read to Someone quickly, and tomorrow I will introduce Read to Someone as a choice. Jeffery loved Read to Someone, and his charting of his reading and tools gave us a visual representation of his work; he was surprised he was able to read for eight minutes.

Day 13

8:55 Round 1 of Daily 5: Introduce Choice with Read to Self, Work on Writing, and Read to Someone! *"Class, I am so excited about our day today. You have learned how to be independent when you do Read to Self, when you do Work on Writing, and when you do Read to Someone. Today you will be completely in charge of the order in which you do them. Some of you may choose Read to Self first, others may choose Work on Writing, while others will choose Read to Someone. Starting today we will limit the number of students who can do Read to Someone during each round to six. So if you choose Read to Someone and six people already checked in with Read to Someone, you will have to make a different choice until the next round. We will be doing three rounds of Daily 5 today.*

"You all know why you are doing each choice and how to work independently. I trust you to be independent during the time you work on your Daily 5 choice, just like you have learned and practiced."

- Have students close their eyes, picture themselves either reading or writing, and think about which they would rather do first.
- Tell students to be ready. When you call their name they will say "Read to Self" or "Work on Writing" or "Read to Someone." As they call their choice, use the check-in sheet and record it.
- During this time, meet individually with students to assess and to set goals.
- When stamina runs out, sound signal and return to gathering area.
- Group check-in: How did it go? Fill in stamina chart (see page 46).

Lesson Plans for Launching the Daily 5 and CAFE (continued)

9:20 Focus Lesson: Your Specific Reading Skill/Strategy; Brain Break

9:30 Round 2 of Daily 5
- Students check in with Read to Self, Work on Writing, or Read to Someone. If they choose the same thing twice, gently remind them to make a different choice.
- Meet individually with students to assess and to set goals.
- When stamina runs out, sound signal and return to gathering area.
- Group check-in: How did it go? Fill in stamina chart (see page 46).

9:50 Focus Lesson: Your Specific Reading Skill/Strategy; Brain Break

10:00 Round 3 of Daily 5
- Students check in with Read to Self, Work on Writing, or Read to Someone. If they choose the same thing twice, gently remind them to make a different choice.
- Meet individually with students to assess and to set goals.
- When stamina runs out, sound signal and return to gathering area.
- Group check-in: How did it go? Fill in stamina chart (see page 46).

10:20 Sharing. Allow a few students a chance to share what they did during Daily 5.

10:25 Review what we did today and what we will do tomorrow.

Teacher Reflective Notes: They love choice. Adding Read to Someone as a choice seemed to be the icing on the cake. They feel so empowered to be able to have an opportunity to work with someone of their choosing. We are now up to three cohesive rounds of Daily 5, where students know what to do each time. We aren't introducing many new behaviors, so I am excited to get into the rhythm of teaching skills and strategies. It feels like we are getting so much done.

Day 14

8:45 Focus Lesson: Your Specific Reading Skill/Strategy; Brain Break

8:55 Round 1 of Daily 5: Introduce Word Work using 10 Steps to Independence
1. "Today we are going to learn to do Word Work. *(Create an I-chart and explain that the I is for independent.)*
2. "We do Word Work because it helps us expand our vocabulary and become better readers, writers, and spellers, and it is *fun*!" *(Write these on the top of the I-chart.)*
3. Record on the I-chart five behaviors that are the most crucial to student success.

Lesson Plans for Launching the Daily 5 and CAFE (continued)

- Work the whole time
- Stay in one spot, except to get and return materials
- Get started right away
- Work quietly
- Work on stamina

4. Have Latoya and Miranda model the most-desirable behaviors. Review the I-chart and ask, "Will Latoya and Miranda become better readers and writers if they do these things?"

5. Have Jake and Clair model the least-desirable behaviors. Review the I-chart and ask, "Will Jake and Clair become better readers and writers if they do these things?" Then have the same students model the most-desirable behaviors. Review the I-chart again and ask the same question. "Will Jake and Clair become better readers and writers if they do these things?"

6. Place students around the room.

7. Practice and build stamina.

8. Stay out of the way.

9. Signal when stamina runs out.

10. Group check-in: How did it go? Fill in stamina chart (see page 46).

9:20 Review **Word-Work I-chart.** Tell students Word Work will also be a choice during Daily 5. So, each round they will have a choice of four of the Daily 5. Explain that they won't have a chance to do all four each day, because there are only three choices each day. So we each have to prioritize. Every day, everyone must do Read to Self and Work on Writing, but for the other round they can choose between Read to Someone and Word Work. Tomorrow we will introduce Listen to Reading, and then they will have five choices but still will only be able to do three things each day.

9:30 Round 2 of Daily 5
- Students check in with Read to Self, Work on Writing, Read to Someone, or Word Work.
- Meet individually with students to assess and to set goals.
- When stamina runs out, sound signal and return to gathering area.
- Group check-in: How did it go? Fill in stamina chart (see page 46).

9:50 Focus Lesson: Your Specific Reading Skill/Strategy; Brain Break

10:00 Round 3 of Daily 5
- Students check in with Read to Self, Work on Writing, Read to Someone, or Word Work.
- Meet individually with students to assess and to set goals.
- When stamina runs out, sound signal and return to gathering area.
- Group check-in: How did it go? Fill in stamina chart (see page 46).

The Daily 5, Second Edition: Fostering Literacy Independence in the Elementary Grades by Gail Boushey and Joan Moser ("The 2 Sisters"). Copyright © 2014. Stenhouse Publishers.

Lesson Plans for Launching the Daily 5 and CAFE (continued)

10:20 Sharing. Allow a few students a chance to share what they did during Daily 5.

10:25 Review what we did today and what we will do tomorrow.

Teacher reflective notes: Now that Read to Someone was introduced, it made sense to me to introduce Word Work and Listen to Reading in these next two days. I have taught all of the foundation lessons, so I know they are ready. As I look at my plans I can see how far the class has come with learning the behaviors of reading and writing and how the reading lessons are taking over my focus lessons. We are on our way.

Day 15

8:45 Introduce Listen to Reading using 10 Steps to Independence. See Day 14, and introduce as you introduced Word Work.

9:20 Focus Lesson: Your Specific Reading Skill/Strategy; Brain Break

9:30 Round 2 of Daily 5
- Students check in with Read to Self, Work on Writing, Read to Someone, Word Work, or Listen to Reading.
- Meet individually with students to assess and to set goals.
- When stamina runs out, sound signal and return to gathering area.
- Group check-in: How did it go? Fill in stamina chart (see page 46).

9:50 Focus Lesson: Your Specific Reading Skill/Strategy; Brain Break

10:00 Round 3 of Daily 5
- Students check in with Read to Self, Work on Writing, Read to Someone, Word Work, or Listen to Reading.
- Meet individually with students to assess and to set goals.
- When stamina runs out, sound signal and return to gathering area.
- Group check-in: How did it go? Fill in stamina chart (see page 46).

10:20 Sharing. Allow a few students a chance to share what they did during Daily 5.

10:25 Review what we did today and what we will do tomorrow.

Teacher reflective notes: All of the Daily 5 are launched. This year it took this class fifteen days, but I know next year it may be longer or shorter, depending on the class that I have. I am reminding myself now that when the class loses stamina during a round, or has a bumpy day, I can go back and review the behaviors and help them set themselves back on the course of independence.

Bibliography

Allington, Richard. 2009. *What Really Matters in Response to Intervention: Research-Based Designs*. Boston, MA: Pearson.

———. 2011. *What Really Matters for Struggling Readers: Designing Research-Based Programs*. 3rd ed. Boston, MA: Pearson.

Allington, Richard L., and Patricia M. Cunningham. 2007. *Schools That Work: Where All Children Read and Write*. 3rd ed. Boston, MA: Allyn & Bacon.

Allington, Richard, and Peter Johnston. 2002. *Reading to Learn: Lessons from Exemplary Fourth-Grade Classrooms*. New York: Guilford.

Anderson, R. C., P. T. Wilson, and L. G. Fielding. 1988. "Growth in Reading and How Children Spend Their Time Outside of School." *Reading Research Quarterly* 23 (3): 285–303.

Atwell, Nancie. 1998. *In the Middle: New Understandings About Writing, Reading, and Learning*. 2nd ed. Portsmouth, NH: Heinemann.

Beaudoin, Marie-Nathalie. 2011. "Respect—Where Do We Start?" *Educational Leadership*, September.

Betts, Emmett. 1946. *Foundations of Reading Instruction*. New York: American Book Company.

———. 1949. "Adjusting Instruction to Individual Needs." In *The Forth-Eighth Yearbook of the National Society for the Study of Education: Part II, Reading in the School*, ed. N. B. Henry. Chicago: University of Chicago Press.

Boushey Gail, and Joan Moser. 2006. *The Daily Five: Fostering Literacy Independence in the Elementary Grades*. Portland, ME: Stenhouse.

———. 2009. *The CAFE Book: Engaging All Students in Daily Literacy Assessment and Instruction*. Portland, ME: Stenhouse.

———. 2013. The Daily CAFE. http://www.thedailycafe.com.

Buckner, Aimee. 2005. *Notebook Know-How: Strategies for the Writer's Notebook*. Portland, ME: Stenhouse.

Calkins, Lucy, Mary Ehrenworth, and Christopher Lehman. 2012. *Pathways to the Common Core: Accelerating Achievement*. Portsmouth, NH: Heinemann.

Coulton, Mia. 2001. *Look at Danny*. Beachwood, OH: Mary Ruth Books.

Covey, Stephen R. 1989. *The Seven Habits of Highly Effective People: Restoring the Character Ethic*. New York: Simon and Schuster.

Farstrup, A. E., and S. J. Samuels, eds. 2011. *What Research Has to Say About Reading Instruction*. 4th ed. Newark, DE: International Reading Association.

Fisher, D., and N. Frey 2008. "Releasing Responsibility." *Educational Leadership* 66 (3): 32–37.

Fisher, Douglas, Nancy Frey, and Diane Lapp. 2009. *In a Reading State of Mind: Brain Research, Teacher Modeling, and Comprehension Instruction*. Newark, DE: International Reading Association.

Fletcher, Ralph, and JoAnn Portalupi. 2013. *What a Writer Needs*. Portland, ME: Stenhouse.

Fletcher, Ralph. 1996. *A Writer's Notebook: Unlocking the Writer Within You*. HarperTrophy.

Gaiman, Neil. 1997. "Where Do You Get Your Ideas?" Neil Gaiman website. http://www.neilgaiman.com/p/Cool_Stuff/Essays/Essays_By_Neil/Where_do_you_get_your_ideas%3F.

Gallagher, Kelly. 2009. *Readicide: How Schools Are Killing Reading and What You Can Do About It*. Portland, ME: Stenhouse.

———. 2011. *Write Like This: Teaching Real-World Writing Through Modeling and Mentor Texts*. Portland, ME: Stenhouse.

Gambrell, L. B., R. M. Wilson, and W. N. Gantt. 1981. "Classroom Observations of Task-Attending Behaviors of Good and Poor Readers." *Journal of Educational Research* 74 (6): 400–404.

Gambrell, Linda. 2011. "Seven Rules of Engagement: What's Most Important to Know About Motivation to Read." *The Reading Teacher* 65 (3): 172–178.

Grinder, Michael. 1995. *ENVoY: Your Personal Guide to Classroom Management*. Battle Ground, WA: Michael Grinder and Associates.

Harwayne, Shelley. 1992. *Lasting Impressions: Weaving Literature into the Writing Workshop*. Portsmouth, NH: Heinemann.

———. 2001. *Writing Through Childhood: Rethinking Process and Product*. Portsmouth, NH: Heinemann.

Howard, Mary. 2009. *RTI from All Sides: What Every Teacher Needs to Know*. Portsmouth, NH: Heinemann.

———. 2012. *Good to Great Teaching: Focusing on the Literacy Work That Matters*. Portsmouth, NH: Heinemann.

Katz, Alan. 2001. *Take Me Out of the Bathtub and Other Silly Dilly Songs*. New York: Margaret K. McElderry Books.

Krashen, Stephen. 2004. *The Power of Reading: Insights from the Research*. Portsmouth, NH: Heinemann.

Leinhardt, Gaea, Naomi Zigmond, and William Cooley. 1981. "Reading Instruction and Its Effects." *American Educational Research Journal* 18 (3): 343–361.

Medina, John. 2009. *Brain Rules: 12 Principles for Surviving and Thriving at Work, Home, and School*. Seattle, WA: Pear Press.

Miller, Debbie. 2013. *Reading with Meaning: Teaching Comprehension in the Primary Grades*. 2nd ed. Portland, ME: Stenhouse.

Miller, Donalyn. 2009. *The Book Whisperer: Awakening the Inner Reader in Every Child*. San Francisco: Jossey-Bass.

Mooney, Margaret. 1990. *Reading to, with, and by Children*. Katonah, NY: Richard C. Owen.

Morrow, Lesley Mandel, Linda Gambrell, and Michael Pressley. 2007. *Best Practices in Literacy Instruction*. New York: Guilford.

Pearson, P. David, and M. C. Gallagher. 1983. "The Instruction of Reading Comprehension." *Contemporary Educational Psychology* 8: 317–344.

Pressley, Michael, Richard Allington, Ruth Wharton-McDonald, Cathy Collins Block, and Lesley Mandel Morrow. 2001. *Learning to Read: Lessons from Exemplary First-Grade Classrooms*. New York: Guilford.

Ray, Katie Wood. 2010. *In Pictures and In Words: Teaching the Qualities of Good Writing Through Illustration Study*. Portsmouth, NH: Heinemann.

Routman, Regie. 2003. *Reading Essentials: The Specifics You Need to Teach Reading Well*. Portsmouth, NH: Heinemann.

———. 2005. *Writing Essentials: Raising Expectations and Results While Simplifying Teaching*. Portsmouth, NH: Heinemann.

Samuels, S. Jay, and Alan E. Farstrup, eds. 2011. *What Research Has to Say About Reading Instruction*. 4th ed. Newark, DE: International Reading Association.

Scientific Learning Corporation. 2008. "Adding Ten Minutes of Reading Time Dramatically Changes Levels of Print Exposure." *Educator's Briefing*. http://www.iowaafterschoolalliance.org/documents/cms/docs/10_minutes.pdf.

Trelease, Jim. 2001. *The Read-Aloud Handbook*. New York: Penguin Books.

Van de Walle, John, and LouAnn H. Lovin. 2006. *Teaching Student-Centered Mathematics: Grades 5–8*. The Van de Walle Professional Mathematics Series. Boston, MA: Pearson.

Index

Page numbers followed by an *f* indicate figures.